LEADER TO LEADER

SPECIAL ISSUE

EXECUTIVE LETTER

The essence of leadership in teams and organizations has certainly evolved over time. It is rooted in the history of management theory from scientific management to administrative management to modern management, as championed by Peter Drucker, and then extended to many of the contemporary authors and concepts of the last quarter-century. The one area often overlooked in this history is the focus on human relations as championed by Dale Carnegie. So it is fitting that *Leader to Leader*, as started by Peter Drucker, would come together with the Dale Carnegie organization to bring you this special issue of *Leader to Leader*. While the current literature tends to advocate that we look beyond one's position and think of leadership in terms of creating results, there is no doubt that leadership is still viewed as position-based in many cases. In this journal, we advocate that effective leadership skills are rooted in developing people and relationships that drive results, and that strong human relations is what gains one a leadership role that may, or may not, be formally recognized on the organization chart.

The focus of this special issue is to help advance the skills advocated by Dale Carnegie—transferable skills such as self-confidence, leadership skills, communication skills, people skills, and attitude control. While such skills form the foundation for professional success, sustained organization impact occurs when leaders move beyond themselves and truly begin to focus on those around them in the organization. This requires those of us who desire to lead to turn from leading ourselves to leading others in ways that impact the organization as a whole. This requires that we look at ourselves through a different lens—that we rethink our role in achieving the most with and through others and build a sense of personal accountability that sets a high standard for those around us. The articles in this issue were selected to help us in this journey from understanding to application to organization impact.

The ever-growing changes in demographics, with baby boomers leaving the Western workforce, and changes in productive power, with the growth of emerging regions, such as the growth of Asia as a leading producer of goods, demonstrates that the need for effective leadership continues to be in high demand. While these changes are often viewed as a crisis in the management ranks, the emerging generation of workers appears to be one more focused on its ability to have impact than to have a position. Thus, the need to consider leadership skills that help drive organization results when one has formal authority and when one does not have a formal position of authority appears to be a growing necessity.

In this special issue of *Leader to Leader*, we will be looking at articles focused on expanding our leadership conversation in five key areas. We start and end with articles on building team confidence and enhancing risk-taking skills. This starts with us as a leader, as we set the tone for how much our team will step forward, be accountable, and drive new ideas. We then look at articles on people and team engagement. This has been a topic of growing interest in recent years. As the content in this journal identifies, too often we look at the engagement level of our team members while neglecting to look for ways to improve our own level of engagement, thus improving overall employee engagement. We will be challenged to rethink engagement, starting with our own commitment. We will also be looking at articles on improving our leadership communication. What is recommended in this issue is that we go beyond simply giving information and focus on how we can increase our influence and results by truly analyzing our approach to effective communication.

In addition, we look at articles that focus on organization leadership skills. Improving in all five major areas discussed in this issue will help us be better leaders. By improving our true leadership focus, we can have a unique impact on those around us. We then conclude the issue by looking at how to deal with the stress of leadership that we face daily. The need to do more, do it better, and do it with fewer resources continues to be the mantra for sustained organization success. Yes, it would be nice to have all of the resources we desire and request, but the reality is that resource constraints can open our thinking to innovative approaches that can benefit all. Our leadership opportunity is to work within our team to bring out the best in each person, connect individual activity with strategic direction, and lead up, down, and around us in ways that truly impact the entire organization. The articles provided here suggest ways of thinking, acting, and leading that help us make the most of our opportunities.

The continued relevance of Dale Carnegie's principles for effective communication and human relations demonstrates the ongoing human desire to engage and influence others. As we prepare to meet organization needs in an ever-changing competitive environment, it is important that we connect with teams, partners, contractors, and customers in new and productive ways. We trust that your Dale Carnegie experience, supplemented with this reading selection, will aid you in your journey from individual success to sustained organization impact.

Kevin J. Sensenig, Ph.D., RODP
Vice-President & Global Brand Champion
Dale Carnegie Training

Thomas H. Gilmore
Master Trainer
Dale Carnegie Training

This special Leader to Leader issue has been prepared exclusively for Dale Carnegie Training. Permission to copy: No part of this issue may be reproduced in any form without permission in writing from the Leader to Leader Institute and Jossey-Bass. For inquiries, write Permissions Dept., c/o John Wiley & Sons, Inc., 111 River Street, Hoboken, NJ 07030 or visit www.wiley.com/go/permissions. Leader to Leader (print ISSN 1087-8149, on-line ISSN 1531-5355) is published quarterly by the Leader to Leader Institute and Wiley Subscription Services, Inc., A Wiley Company, at Jossey-Bass, 989 Market St., San Francisco, CA 94103-1741. Copyright © 2010 by the Leader to Leader Institute. All rights reserved. **For more information or to subscribe, please contact Leader to Leader, Jossey-Bass, A Wiley Imprint, 989 Market Street, 5th Floor, San Francisco, CA 94103-1741; 888.378.2537; jbsubs@jbp.com.**

THE FIVE INTELLIGENCES OF LEADERSHIP

by Clint Sidle

Leadership is a particular way of approaching life, one of being committed to a lifelong process of growing toward human fulfillment. Framed in this way leadership becomes a vehicle for personal transformation as well as an agent for positive change. Perhaps more than in any other era of our history, the social, environmental, and ethical challenges of our time demand such a perspective on leadership. We need more leaders who are inspired not only by doing well for themselves but also by doing good in the world.

But how do we develop such leaders? Although leadership development has received a great deal of attention in recent years, we still lack a common framework for understanding what leadership is and how it is developed. As James McGregor Burns once put it, "Leadership is one of the most often studied yet least understood phenomena on earth."

A number of years ago, I came across a unifying framework that I found intuitive and compelling, both for its elegant simplicity and for its inherent potential for addressing human fulfillment. This framework emerged from the study of indigenous cultures across the world—Native American, African, Celtic, and Tibetan, among others. Anthropologists and psychologists found these cultures share unmistakable similarities in their views of what it takes to be an effective human

being: four or five archetypal intelligences portrayed through the cardinal directions of the compass. More commonly known as a mandala, or medicine wheel, this ancient framework provides a guide for personal growth and effectiveness that has withstood the test of time for thousands of years.

Each direction represents a particular intelligence for learning, relating, and living in harmony with the world. Taken as a whole, the directions symbolize perfection and balance; they provide a guide for understanding the self and realizing one's full human potential. An individual is held to have been born into a single direction, and so entered the world dominated by a root preference. Yet the purpose of life is to seek self-understanding and grow to completeness by accessing the intelligence of the other directions, and in so doing reach a place of balance and goodness from which to lead and influence others. (See Figure 1.)

According to the ancient paradigm, each intelligence has both a wisdom aspect and a shadow aspect. Wisdom turns into shadow when it is used to validate the ego and serve self-interest—usually because of a fear or insecurity. As a result, people tend to overplay their view to the point of turning a strength into a weakness, creating obstacles to developing personal influence,

        Reprinted from Leader to Leader Number 43, Winter 2007

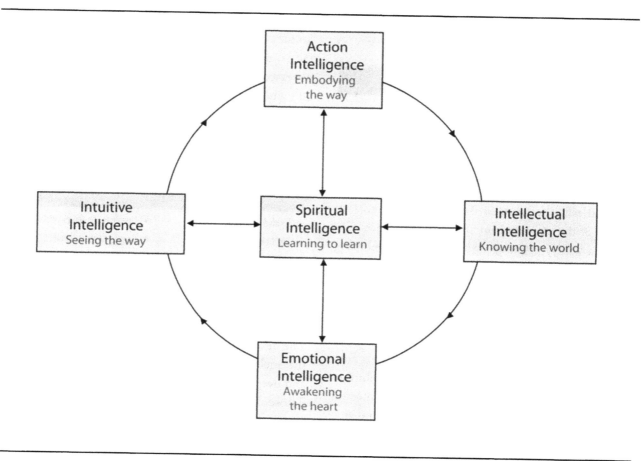

FIGURE 1. THE FIVE INTELLIGENCES OF LEADERSHIP

learning, and effective relationships. Thus the framework provides insight not only into personal effectiveness but also personal derailment.

Although no perfect parallels exist, the similarities between the five intelligences and the research of 20th-century psychologists and management thinkers are remarkable. There are clear parallels, for example, with the four Jungian personality types, the five dimensions of the Five Factor Model used in modern psychological research, and much of recent management literature, including the work of Peter Senge, Kouzes and Posner, and Peter Koestenbaum and others. It seems, then, that our modern age is rediscovering this ancient wisdom.

The key difference, however, is the utter simplicity and intuitive appeal the five intelligences have for under-

standing leadership and how to develop leaders who do well while doing good in the world.

The Five Intelligences of Leadership

EAST: Intellectual intelligence—knowing the world. The first is intellectual intelligence. People with strong intellects seek, acquire, and hold knowledge.

The influence of leaders rests in part on their expertise and their intellectual grasp of their profession and industry. Their technical skill, rational thought, and objective, data-driven minds enable them to see reality clearly and objectively. They lead by being attentive to detail, asking critical questions, sharing their insights, and teaching others. They also capture and share their expertise for the prosperity of all. *This is leader as expert, and also leader as coach and mentor.*

Wisdom	
• Intellectual curiosity	• Focus on the real, present, specific, and concrete
• Logic and rationality	
• Objectivity	• Business and technical knowledge and acumen
• Methodicalness and order	

Orit Gadiesh, chairman of Bain & Company, is an example of the powers of intellectual intelligence. Gadiesh is a widely acknowledged expert in developing corporate strategy, but she gets results for her clients by first establishing a set of facts as the point of departure. For her, "Information is the foundation to the right solution, one that must be practical and collectively obtained." For a strategy to be successful, it must be based on facts and not wishful thinking. She is concerned with finding the truth and developing solutions grounded in that truth. Therefore she spends most of her time listening to clients, asking questions, and analyzing data to develop an intellectual grasp of the situation. And she engages every level of the organization in that process so that understanding is shared. "It means working with people at all levels, building a partnership that gives clients ownership, and sometimes telling them what they do not want to hear."

The shadow of intellectual intelligence comes from a fear of being wrong or not knowing. When something arises outside the current range of understanding,

Wisdom turns into shadow when it is used to validate the ego and serve self-interest.

people of this type feel thwarted, even threatened. So they hold on to their view and become rigid, righteous, and overly critical of others. They become obsessed with detail, lose sight of the big picture, and when pushed they become annoyed, even angry. Research shows that rigidity, insensitivity, and inability to see the big picture are common reasons for leadership derailment.

Shadow	
• Fixated and tight	• Unable to see the big picture
• Rigid and inflexible	• Bogged down in detail
• Uncomfortable with ambiguity	• Apparent insensitivity
• Subject to analysis paralysis	

SOUTH: Emotional intelligence—awakening the heart. The next is emotional intelligence. It is the place where the intellectual stimulus of the first direction is enriched and deepened through feeling and emotional reaction. Those dominant in this intelligence are focused on people and forging strong and supportive relationships. For them, *how* things are done is just as important as *what* is done. They are able to recognize and manage their own feelings and emotions and those of others. They care about people and are socially skilled: good listeners, communicators, networkers, and team players. They are also concerned with helping others and empowering them to be the best they can be. *This is leader as servant and leader as a people person.*

Wisdom	
• Emotionally aware and empathic	• Values driven
• Good at relationship building	• Service oriented
• Team player, collaborative	• Good listener and communicator

Mike Krzyzewski, coach of the Duke Blue Devils basketball team, provides a great example of emotional intelligence. Coach K says he does not coach winning the game; rather, he coaches a winning culture. For him, coaching is not just teaching basketball—it is about values, honesty, teamwork, and transcending self-interest to support others in serving a greater cause.

Vision serves to uplift aspirations, foster commitment, and galvanize others.

As an example of his team orientation, he tells the story of one early season where two freshmen were late for the team bus. No one knew where they were; no one called. Eventually they arrived and after hearing that they overslept, Coach K wondered why others had not checked up on them. So rather than reprimand them, he talked to the team as a whole about what it means to be a team. "If one of us is late," he told them, "then we are all late." For Krzyzewski, teamwork is about mutual respect and caring for one another, not simply winning the game.

The shadow of the emotional intelligence arises out of a fear of inadequacy, and manifests as feeling that is turned inward—other-feeling turns into self-feeling. So, whereas shadow intellectuals are hung up on their *ideas of things*, shadow emotional intelligence people get hung up on their *feelings of themselves*. They take themselves too seriously, becoming dependent on others for approval and overly sensitive to criticism. And since harmony is so important to them, they also avoid conflict. Unassertiveness, oversensitivity, and dependence are their key derailment factors.

Shadow	
• Oversensitivity	• Unassertiveness
• Prone to take things personally	• Apt to feel guilty about differences
• Dependent	
• Avoidance of conflict	• Excessively proud

WEST: Intuitive intelligence—seeing the way. The west is about intuitive intelligence and the vision for attaining the highest goals in life. People with strong intuitive intelligence are able to assimilate the intellectual and emotional impressions of the first two directions to discern what is most important and to form a conceptual understanding. They are able to see the big picture and to think creatively and strategically in a way that helps them see the opportunities and the possibilities. They also have a clear purpose and vision for what they are doing, and that vision serves to uplift aspirations, foster commitment, and galvanize others. This is leader as visionary, leader as architect, or leader as designer.

Wisdom	
• Creative and innovative	• Change-oriented
• Able to connect the dots and see the big picture	• Able to see what is most important
	• Inspiring and uplifting
• Conceptual, abstract thinker	• Spontaneous

John Chambers, CEO of Cisco Systems, is a good example of an intuitive leader. Chambers is considered one of the most dynamic and innovative chief executives in the country, and although Cisco has lost some of its luster in the last few years, Chambers has nonetheless left a positive mark. His vision is to build the country's most influential company—"not just successful financially, but successful in changing so many aspects of our lives and developing a supportive culture." He wants Cisco to do for networking what Microsoft did for personal computers and IBM did for mainframes. To get there, his vision is to develop a culture that fosters value-centered management, teamwork, and respect for people. He wants to make Cisco a place where people *want* to come and do good work. "If you take my top managers," he said in an interview, "I know what motivates all of them and what is important to them, and we align their goals with company goals." Chambers, then, not only has vision for his industry and his company, but also for his culture and his people.

The shadow side of intuitive intelligence arises out of a fear of meaninglessness or loss of purpose. Shadow intuitives compensate by constantly pursuing new possibilities. As a result they lose sight of the detail, lack follow-through, and compulsively chase dreams as they jump from one idea to the next. Their distractions spread them too thin and leave no time for their discriminatory faculties to function. They derail from inattention to detail and inability to maintain focus and see something to completion.

Shadow	
• Unfocused	• Inattentive to detail
• Overcommitted	• Easily bored
• Impulsive and addictive	• Impractical
• Unable to follow through	

NORTH: Action intelligence—embodying the way. The intelligence of the north is action intelligence. People with action intelligence are driven, task- and result-oriented, and able to get things done. They assume control, challenge the process, take risks, and experiment to make things happen. More important, they walk the talk, model the way, and align their actions with their words and deeds. *This is leader as model, or leader by example.*

Wisdom	
• Task and result oriented	• Disciplined
• Courageous and willing to take risks	• Authentic—walks the talk
• Full of drive and ambition	• Strong and persevering

Aaron Feuerstein, former CEO of Malden Mills, makers of Polartec, is a remarkable example of action intelligence. Feuerstein made news in 1995, when a fire burned most of Malden Mills to the ground, leaving 3,000 people out of work. Rather than lose his employees and devastate the economy of the small town, Feuerstein spent millions of his own money to keep all 3,000 employees on the payroll for three months while he rebuilt the company. Where he could have cashed in

Feuerstein's stand on doing the right thing remains an example for others.

on insurance settlements or sold the company, instead he invested millions to save livelihoods and the local economy. In contrast to others of our time, Feuerstein lived up to his words and took care of his people. He is dedicated to being clear on what is most important to him and acting accordingly. So he did "what was merely the right thing to do." The outpouring of employee and public support were so great that shipments were double within a few weeks after the plant reopening. Malden Mills is still not out of trouble, as the company has refused to follow the industry trend of exporting jobs, but his stand on doing the right thing remains an example for others.

The shadow of the action orientation arises out of fear of being left behind, or of losing control. Action-oriented leaders can become so attached to accomplishing goals that they constantly compare their output to the achievements of others—and become ambitious, aggressive, and controlling to the point of being insensitive and bulldozing. They become busybodies, doing for the sake of doing, and as a result they often charge off in the wrong direction. Insensitivity, abrasiveness, and micromanagement are often hallmarks of a derailed leader.

Shadow	
• Busyness	• Bulldozing
• Excessive competitiveness and aggression	• Tendency to proceed by "ready, fire, aim"
• Insensitivity	• Controlling
• Micromanagement	

CENTER: Spiritual intelligence—learning to learn. Finally there is spiritual intelligence. It is the place of consciousness where the governing urge to learn, grow, and realize our full potential awakens. Effective leaders know themselves and what they have to offer. They have a desire not only to learn but to learn how to learn, to take charge of their own development. They know themselves, and they are open, candid, and humble in their striving to grow and develop. They are optimistic and feel empowered to make the most of any experience. This makes them calm and serene, because situations approached in this manner become workable. This also makes them agile and able to adapt to changing situations. *This is leader as learner.*

Wisdom	
• Self-awareness and understanding	• Openness and candor
• Personal agility and balance	• Calm
• Eagerness to learn	• Optimism

Colin Powell displays the powers of the learner. The child of a humble immigrant family in the Bronx, Powell had an extraordinary career of both professional success and personal contribution. Powell is noted for his self-effacing style and apparent ease in dealing with crisis and power, but what may be most important is the way his leadership is distinguished by what he calls "optimism as a force multiplier." For him, optimism is not based on our external reality; rather, it is determined by how we regulate our inner world. It is an attitude toward life that encourages us to continue where pessimists would give up. It is not unbounded; rather, it is disciplined. For Powell, good leaders ground their optimism in an awareness and knowledge of themselves and the situation, and are able to learn and adapt based on their experience. This optimism becomes a "force multiplier" when the seemingly impossible is achieved and motivates people to even greater standards in the future.

The shadow of the spiritual intelligence arises out of a fear of powerlessness over life. The shadow is disempowering, making people feel victimized and wanting to withdraw from taking responsibility for life. In this case people want to hang out and not be bothered, leaving the details of life unattended to, uncared for,

Awareness helps us see our patterns, and compassion helps us see their impact on others.

and neglected. They shrink from reality and lose focus on who they are, and they tend to become complacent and ignore important signals or feedback in their lives that would call on them to change, grow, and develop. In effect, they fall asleep.

Shadow	
• Doubt	• Dullness
• Spaciness	• Denial
• Complacency	• Victim mentality

Conclusion

Having taken this tour, we begin to see why balance among all five intelligences is important to personal effectiveness and leadership. Each direction offers a unique and important way of knowing and relating to the world; taken together, they move us toward our full potential. In this sense, the five intelligences are not only a framework for understanding self but also a framework for understanding learning. Action intelligence, for instance, without the compassion of emotional intelligence could be insensitive. Likewise, action without the perspective of intuitive intelligence could be misdirected. And finally, action without the hard questions of intellectual intelligence could be premature. All sides of the compass are necessary for effective learning and action.

The five intelligences also offer a five-step action learning cycle leading to progressively higher states of knowledge and action. Intellectual intelligence takes in information objectively; emotional intelligence adds depth to that experience by reacting with feelings of pleasure, pain, or indifference; intuitive intelligence assimilates this data and conceptualizes a plan for action; action intelligence follows through by closing the gap between idea and reality, and spiritual intelligence reflects on the lessons learned for the next cycle.

Finally, this framework also underscores the importance of selflessness for achieving this balance. The shadow is transmuted into wisdom through openness and having the courage to let go of this solid sense of self, step through the fear, and dare to try a new view. Instead of negating or ignoring fears, fears are turned into vehicles for personal growth. Openness is a combination of awareness and compassion. Awareness helps us see our patterns, and compassion helps us see their impact on others. Together they help us suspend the sense of self and open us to new possibilities. In the process we move from selfishness toward selflessness, become more whole and complete, and learn to lead from a place of basic goodness.

The basic strategies for practicing and developing the different intelligences and transmuting the shadow into wisdom are the following:

Intelligence	Wisdom	Shadow	Strategy
Intellectual	Knowing the world	Tightness	Objectivity
Emotional	Awakening the heart	Oversensitivity	Equanimity
Intuitive	Seeing the way	Compulsive desire	Judgment
Action (Volitional)	Embodying the way	Competitiveness	Self-discipline
Spiritual (Consciousness)	Learning to learn	Dullness	Awareness

Thus the wisdom of the five directions provides us with a useful framework for understanding leadership as well as a balanced and integrated path for personal growth and development—one that results in the wisdom and balance necessary for acting in the most effective manner for the benefit of all.

Clint Sidle is an author and consultant, and also serves as director of the Roy H. Park Leadership Fellows Program in the Johnson School of Management at Cornell University. He has consulted with a wide spectrum of organizations in the business and nonprofit worlds, including Meredith Corp., Corning Inc., Citigroup, ATT, Kelloggs, Borg Warner, the New York State Bar Association, the American Red Cross, and a number of higher education institutions. He is the author of "The Leadership Wheel: Five Steps to Individual and Organizational Greatness," which expands on and applies the principles presented in this article. Visit his site at www.clintsidle.org.

THE TRANSFORMATION FROM "I" TO "WE"

Bill George and Andrew McLean

We've all seen the traits in our bosses, subordinates, and colleagues: leaders who have the right skills, use the latest management tools, articulate the right messages with the most popular buzzwords, and hone the right strategies. But underneath something seems to be missing. Followers respond with caution because these leaders always seem to be promoting themselves. Supervisors are worried, but can't pin down what's wrong. Even concerned friends keep their distance. While all the pieces seem to be there, these leaders are never able to rally enthusiastic support from their teams. Leadership, it seems, involves more than a set of skills. But what?

For the last several years, with the full engagement of our colleagues Peter Sims and Diana Mayer, we have been investigating leadership development from the ground up and the top down, culminating with a study of 125 authentic leaders known for their success, effectiveness, and integrity. (This research forms the basis for Bill George's new book, *True North: Discover Your Authentic Leadership,* written with Peter Sims.) We sought to answer the question, What propels leaders as they move from being individual contributors to effective, authentic leaders?

In these in-person interviews, which averaged 75 minutes in length, we asked leaders to tell us the reasons for their success and how they developed as leaders. What we learned came as a big surprise. Contrary to the competence-based approaches to leadership development of the past three decades, these leaders did not cite any characteristics, styles, or traits that led to their success. In fact, they preferred *not* to talk about their success at all. Instead, they focused on their life stories, and the people and experiences that shaped them as leaders. We learned that their stories had ups and downs, and that many of them had to overcome great personal difficulties en route to becoming successful leaders—difficulties that made the business challenges they faced pale by comparison.

What nearly all of these leaders had in common was a transformative passage through which they recognized

They realized that leadership is not about getting others to follow them.

that leadership was not about their success at all. As a consequence of their experiences, they realized that leadership is not about getting others to follow them. Rather, they gained the awareness that the essence of their leadership is aligning their teammates around a shared vision and values and empowering them to step up and lead. For some of these leaders the difficult experiences occurred at a young age, but it took a triggering event many years later to cause them to reframe their experiences and find their calling to lead authentically.

"When you become a leader, your challenge is to inspire others, develop them, and create change through them," Jaime Irick, a West Point alumnus and emerging leader at General Electric, explained to us. "You've got to flip that switch and understand that it's about serving the folks on your team."

We call this the transformation from "I" to "We."

The Long Journey to Transformation

Leaders we studied began their careers with a primary focus on themselves—their performance, achievements, and rewards. As they entered the world of work, they envisioned themselves in the image of an all-conquering hero, able to change the world for the better. As shown in Figure 1, this first phase of the leadership development journey usually lasts from birth until around 30. For most leaders, the first three decades of their lives are spent gathering experience, skills, and relationships before leadership opportunities present themselves.

One might think that the archetypal hero would be a natural model for an organization's leader. Yet in our in-

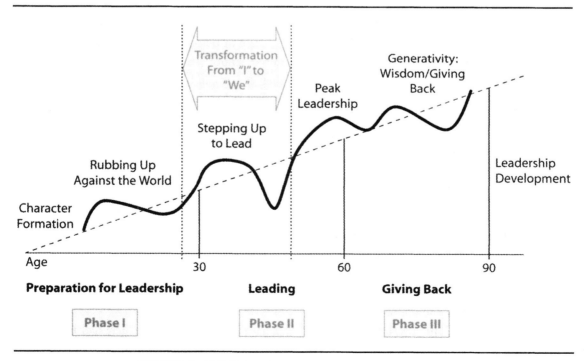

FIGURE 1. THE TRANSFORMATION FROM "I" TO "WE"

terviews with authentic leaders, the hero role turned out to be representative only of their early development. Initially, doing impressive deeds, facing challenges alone, and gaining notice—the hero's job—seemed the best route to success. This is a perfectly natural embarkation point for leaders. After all, so much early success in life depends upon individual efforts, from grades earned in school to performance in individual sports to initial jobs. Admissions offices and employers examine those achievements most closely and use them to make comparisons.

That stage is useful, but many find it hard to move beyond it. As leaders are promoted from individual roles to management, they can start to believe they are being recognized for their ability to get others to follow. "We spend our early years trying to be the best," says Irick. "To get into West Point or General Electric, you have to be the best. That is defined by what you can do on your own—your ability to be a phenomenal analyst or consultant or do well on a standardized test."

In spite of the rewards for heroic performance, most leaders we interviewed reached a point on their journeys when their way forward was blocked or their worldview was turned upside down. They found that their journey was not following the straight ascending path in Figure 1, but more resembled the ups and downs traced around it. Their successes were mirrored by challenges, as dips followed the highs.

It was the lessons from the difficult periods that seeded the transformation from "I" to "We." Success reinforces what leaders do at an early stage. Challenges force them to rethink their approach. At some point, all leaders have to rethink what their life and leadership are all about. They may start to question: "Am I good enough?" "Why can't I get this team to achieve the goals I have set forth?" Or they may have a personal experience that causes them to realize that there is more to life than getting to the top.

It is crucial to emphasize that Figure 1 is one idealized depiction of the course and timing of the transformation from "I" to "We." In the examples that follow, readers will note first that a transformative experience may come at any point in a leader's life.

For some, the transformation from "I" to "We" results from the positive experience of having a wise mentor or a unique opportunity at a young age. But as much as we all want positive experiences like these, transformations for most leaders result from going through a crucible. In *Geeks and Geezers,* Warren Bennis and Robert Thomas describe the concept of the crucible as an experience that tests leaders to their limits. A crucible can be triggered by events such as confronting a difficult situation at work, receiving critical feedback, or losing your job. Or it may result from a painful personal experience such as divorce, illness, or the death of a loved one.

Transformative Experiences in Leadership Development

The examples we present here, which we were given in the course of our interviews, show the many ways in which leaders can be transformed and that the process can sometimes be protracted. What they have in common is that the leaders each came face to face with the limits of what they had done before, and that they confronted the necessity to change. These limits can be experienced on or off the job, and the necessity to change can be fostered by others or it may be purely existential.

Getting Tough Feedback

One of the hardest things for high-performance leaders to do is to see themselves as others see them. When they receive critical feedback, especially if it is unexpected, their first response tends to be defensive—to challenge the validity of the criticism or the critics themselves. If they can get past those feelings and process the criticism objectively, however, constructive feedback can trigger a fundamental reappraisal of their leadership.

"When you become a leader, you've got to flip that switch."

At some point, all leaders have to rethink what their life and leadership are all about.

That's what Doug Baker Jr. learned when he was rising through the ranks of Minnesota-based Ecolab. After working in marketing in Germany for three years, Baker moved to North Carolina as deputy head of a newly acquired company. To integrate his team, Baker hired a coach to conduct 360-degree assessments and facilitate group sessions. "I elected to be first to go through the high-impact leadership program."

At 34, Baker saw himself as a fast-rising star, moving rapidly from one leadership role to the next. "I had become, frankly, fairly arrogant and was pushing my own agenda." Then he got the results from the 360-degree process, in which his colleagues told him all this and more. "It was a cathartic experience. I got a major dose of criticism I didn't expect," he said.

> As part of this process, I went away for five days with a dozen strangers from different companies and shared my feedback with them. Since I had been so understanding in this session, I expected people to say, "How could your team possibly give you that feedback?" Instead, I got the same critical feedback from this new group.
>
> It was as if someone flashed a mirror in front of me at my absolute worst. What I saw was horrifying, but it was also a great lesson. After that, I did a lot of soul-searching about what kind of leader I was going to be. I talked to everyone on my Ecolab team about what I had learned, telling them, "Let's have a conversation. I need your help."

Meanwhile, Baker's division was challenged by a larger competitor who threatened to take away its business with McDonald's, which accounted for the bulk of its revenues. When he forecast a significant shortfall from his financial plan, the corporate CEO traveled to North Carolina to find out what was going on. Asked by the CEO to commit to saving the McDonald's business and getting back on plan, Baker refused to give him any assurances. This raised the CEO's ire, but Baker held his ground. Reflecting on his candor in confronting his powerful leader, Baker commented, "I'd rather have a bad meeting than a bad life."

> If we had lost McDonald's, it would be embarrassing for me, but it was all these folks in the plant who were really going to be hurt. There was unemployment all over North Carolina as many factories were shutting down. If they don't have a job here, they don't have a job, period. Suddenly, you find the cause is a call to the heart. Saving the McDonald's account created a lot of energy and fortunately, we retained the business. It was a traumatic time, but ultimately a great learning experience for me.

Doug Baker's critical feedback came at just the right time. On the verge of becoming overly self-confident and thinking that leadership was about his success, the criticisms brought him back to earth. They enabled him to realize his role as a leader was to unite the people in his organization around a common purpose, and the challenge of saving the McDonald's account provided a rallying point for that unity. This experience paved the way for him to eventually become CEO of Ecolab.

Gail McGovern, a former telecommunications executive who is currently a business school professor, told of struggling with her leadership. "Within one month I went from being the best programmer to the worst supervisor that Bell of Pennsylvania had," she said.

> It's unbelievable how bad I was. I didn't know how to delegate. When somebody would have a question about something they were working on, I'd pick it up and do it. My group was not accomplishing anything because I was on the critical path of everything. My boss and mentor saw that we were imploding and did an amazing thing. He gave me every new project that came in. It was unreal.

At 4:30 my team would leave, and I'd be working day and night trying to dig through this stuff.

Finally, I couldn't take it any longer. I went into his office and stamped my foot like a five-year-old. "It's not fair. I have the work of 10 people." He said calmly, "Look out there. You've got 10 people. Put them to work." It was such a startling revelation. I said sheepishly, "I get it."

As difficult as it is to take in, feedback provides the opportunity to make the transformation from focusing on ourselves to understanding how we can be effective motivators and leaders of others, just as Baker and McGovern did. This requires letting go and trusting others.

Hitting the Wall

Many leaders have an experience at work that dramatically tests their sense of self, their values, or their assumptions about their future or career. We call this "hitting the wall," because the experience resembles a fast-moving race car hitting the wall of the track—but it's something most rising leaders experience at least once in their careers.

General Electric CEO Jeff Immelt was a fast-rising star in his mid-30s when he faced his toughest challenge. Asked to return to GE's plastics business as head of world sales and marketing, he had reservations about accepting the move because it was not a promotion. Jack Welch told him, "I know this isn't what you want to do, but this is a time when you serve the company."

Facing stiff competition, the division had entered into several long-term fixed-price contracts with key customers, including U.S. automakers, when a spike of inflation sent the division's costs soaring. Immelt's operation missed its operating profit target by $30 million, or 30 percent of its budget. He tried to increase prices, but progress was slow, as Immelt's actions caused the division's crucial relationship with General Motors to deteriorate.

This only intensified the pressure on Immelt to produce results and forced Welch to resolve the issues by talking to GM CEO Roger Smith. Welch did not hesitate to reach down to pepper Immelt with questions by phone. Immelt recalled the year as a remarkably difficult one until he and his team could start to turn the business around.

Nobody wants to be around somebody going through a low period. In times like that you've got to be able to draw from within. Leadership is one of these great journeys into your own soul.

Jeff Immelt was under enormous pressure to deliver immediate results, but he withstood the pressure to compromise and took the long-term course of getting the business back on track. Immelt's success in leading this turnaround prepared him to become Welch's successor, where he has faced much greater pressure but has stayed the course, holding to his beliefs and his strategy to build GE for the next decade.

Steve Rothschild was on the move at General Mills. He created the Yoplait yogurt business in the United States and put it on course to become a $1 billion business. Promoted to executive vice president while still in his 30s, he faced many new challenges. After eight years in this role, Rothschild became restless. He felt like a man in the middle, missing the satisfaction of leading his own team. He also disagreed with the company's direction, judging it had to become more global. Rothschild faced up to the reality that he was marching to a different drummer and wasn't enjoying his work. After some reflection, he decided it was time to leave General Mills. "I was stuck in a job I no longer enjoyed. I needed to feel alive again," he said.

Using his own money, he founded Twin Cities RISE! Its mission is to provide employers with skilled workers by training unemployed and underemployed adults, especially African American men, for skilled jobs that pay a wage of at least $20,000 per year with benefits.

Leaving General Mills was a godsend for me. It allowed me to explore things that were underneath my skin and in my soul and gave me the opportunity to refocus on my marriage and family. Since leaving, my relationships with my family have become much

Transformations take many forms.

closer and deeper. Making this move has made me a more complete person, more fulfilled and happier.

Leaders react to experiences like these in one of three ways. They can remain stuck in their old ways and continue in their current positions, usually with negative consequences. Or the experience can be sobering as leaders like Immelt realize they are not superhuman and have to face difficult trials like everyone else. This enables them to be more empathic and empowering to the people around them. Finally, they may decide, as Steve Rothschild did, that fundamental changes are required in their lives and wind up pursuing different career directions. In either case, such a crucible provides the basis for the transformation from "I" to "We."

Seeing Life Whole

When you meet Carlson Companies' CEO Marilyn Carlson Nelson for the first time, you are struck by her warmth, her zest for life, and her optimism that any problem can be solved by inspiring people to step up and lead. Yet hers is a more complex story. As if it were yesterday, she vividly recalls learning the news of her daughter's death. "My husband and I heard one morning that our beautiful 19-year-old Juliet had been killed in an automobile accident."

> That's the most profound test we've ever had, a test of our faith and our personal relationship. I lost my faith at the time and felt angry with God. But God didn't abandon me and didn't let me go. I discovered how valuable every day is and how valuable each person is. I decided to make whatever time I had left meaningful so that time that Juliet didn't have would be well spent. My husband and I vowed to use every tool at hand as an opportunity to give back or a way to make life better for people. They are all human beings with one short time on Earth.

Soon after her daughter's death, Nelson joined Carlson Companies full-time, where she has devoted herself to empowering the organization's 150,000 employees to serve its customers in a highly personalized manner. Twenty years later she remains dedicated to the vow she made to make life better for people. In 2006, she was named one of "America's Best Leaders" by *U.S. News & World Report*.

Only when leaders stop focusing on their personal ego needs are they able to develop other leaders.

Virgin Mobile USA CEO Dan Schulman described how his sister's death transformed his attitudes toward leadership. "Before my sister died, I was focused on moving up in AT&T. I was upwardly oriented and insecure. Often I took credit that wasn't mine to claim."

> My sister's death was the first time I had been dealt a giant blow. I loved her immensely. When death happens so young and cuts a life short, a lot of things you thought were important aren't important at all. When she died, I decided, "I am going to be who I am." I wanted to spend more time with my folks and my brother, rather than moving up the corporate ladder.

> At that point I didn't care if I got credit for anything and became quick to credit everyone else. As team leader, I focused only on getting the job done in the best way. As a result, our teams became much more functional than they were before. All of a sudden, my career started to shoot up.

Both Nelson and Schulman used the trauma of the death of their loved ones to rethink what their lives and leadership were about. With a newfound sense of mission, they reoriented their leadership into focusing on others.

Guiding the Transformation

The transformation from "I" to "We" is the point where leaders step out of the hero's journey and embark on the leader's journey. Their crucible experiences cause leaders to reorganize the meaning of their experience and make a commitment to goals larger than themselves.

The transformation can take many forms. In addition to breaking a leader out of the hero's journey, transformative experiences can also shape leaders' values, sense of compassion, sense of purpose, reliance on support networks, and commitment to self-discipline—all elements that are necessary to leaders' authenticity and effectiveness.

We single out the transition from "I" to "We" because that transformation stems from experiences that place leaders in the space of a powerful paradox. To recover from a life-changing setback requires the continued deployment of the competitive drive and skills that leaders have been working to master to that point. At the same time, their experiences force them to be humble.

This newfound humility stems from the recognition that leadership is not about them. This recognition propels them into the next stages of leadership development as the hero's journey is left behind and the leader's journey begins.

Only when leaders stop focusing on their personal ego needs are they able to develop other leaders. They feel less competitive with talented peers and subordinates and are more open to other points of view, enabling them to make better decisions. As they overcome their need to control everything, they learn that people are more interested in working with them. A lightbulb goes on as they recognize the unlimited potential of empowered leaders working together toward a shared purpose.

Bill George is professor of management practice at Harvard Business School and the former chairman and CEO of Medtronic. His latest book is "True North: Discover Your Authentic Leadership," written with Peter Sims. His earlier book, "Authentic Leadership: Rediscovering the Secret to Creating Lasting Value," was a BusinessWeek best-seller and selected as one of the "Best Business Books of 2003 and 2004" by the Economist magazine. He serves on the boards of ExxonMobil, Goldman Sachs, and Novartis.

Andrew McLean is an independent consultant and adjunct faculty member at Bentley College in Boston. His research has appeared in the Harvard Business Review and Strategy and Leadership. He was research director for the True North leadership development study while a research associate at Harvard Business School.

EMPLOYEE ENGAGEMENT:

BEYOND THE FAD AND INTO THE EXECUTIVE SUITE

Theresa M. Welbourne

When you hear the word *engagement*, you might think of long-term commitment, marriage, diamonds, family, and celebration; however, today the word is associated with one of the hottest topics in management. Everyone seems to be on the path to getting their employees engaged. The claim has been made that engagement is needed for higher levels of firm performance, and consultant studies estimate that only 14 percent to 30 percent of employees are engaged at work.

But to date, despite a surge in interest in improving engagement, people still disagree about what employee engagement is, how to go about getting it, and what it looks like when it is achieved. Additionally, with all the attention given to reported levels of low employee engagement, there are few if any statistics on what a realistic level of engagement should be for employees overall and for various subgroups of workers.

In particular, very little attention has been given to the engagement levels of the people running organiza-tions—the leadership and management teams. Regardless of what definition of engagement is used, if it is something organizations are trying to do to employees rather than a quality that leaders are demonstrating through example, the interventions associated with engagement will fail.

In this article, I focus on the context and behaviors of employee engagement. I do this to understand what may be causing the reported low levels of engagement and to spell out the critical role that leaders play in improving performance through employee engagement. To study the framework for engagement, I introduce the role-based model of performance. This model spells out five specific roles that employees occupy at work—and the links between these roles and improved firm performance tell the story of what happens when employees become engaged at work.

Knowing the relationship between employee behavior and firm performance, while simultaneously understanding the context in which leaders are running their

Reprinted from Leader to Leader Number 44, Spring 2007

organizations, it becomes clear that engagement is not going to be a quick fix. Leaders face challenges of being engaged themselves, getting structural barriers out of the way of engagement, and dealing with an employee contract that does not support engagement at work.

Origins of Employee Engagement

Employee engagement has appeared on the management scene in a big way fairly recently. A review of recent history helps to clarify why it is so popular today. Prior to the 1980s, employers expected loyalty to the organization, and in exchange for that commitment, they offered lifetime employment. Then in the 1980s organizations started to change that contract.

With increased global competition, employers needed to be more flexible in their deployment of employees. Plants were closed and then reopened in countries where wages were lower, and as business became global, leaders needed more control over wage and benefit costs to compete effectively. Employees learned the hard way (through layoffs) that loyalty was no longer rewarded. College seniors were told they could no longer expect long-term employment, and career progress became viewed as a spiral instead of a ladder. The rules of the game changed, and leaders in business initiated the evolution.

The workforce has changed. Employers wanted it to change; however, in many cases, they did not quite want *everyone* to change. The new employment contract backfired. High-quality talent left organizations, and productivity suffered. Skilled employees were not willing to put in overtime and extra effort, and employers started to see increases in productivity slow down. This situation created the need for something new, and at least one of the initiatives was employee engagement.

The driving need today is for business to continue to improve productivity in a global environment where continuous change is making it difficult to compete. This desire to do more is combined with the mandate to do so with less, and one of the only outlets left for

Employees learned the hard way that loyalty was no longer rewarded.

making this happen is employees. However, given the employee contract as it has been redefined, it is not easy for employers to snap their fingers and simply get employees to do more. Thus, the employee engagement movement arrived as a way to solve this problem. The experts claim that engaged employees do more; therefore, to get more out of less, the logic would be that managers simply need to engage their people.

Behavior, Not Attitudes

Many case studies detail how efforts to improve employee engagement can improve firm performance outcomes (such as sales and profitability) and other outcomes such as absenteeism, customer service scores, and more. However, these data are primarily focused on employee attitudes (that is, the degree to which employees describe themselves as motivated, inspired, feeling liked by coworkers, having opportunities to excel, and so on), and they do not spell out the process by which these employee attitudes lead to changed behaviors or what specific actions drive performance. In today's environment, where the employee contract has evolved considerably, the process by which we expect engagement to happen needs to be fully understood so that managers can change contract terms or other context issues to enable full employee engagement.

The only way to improve employee engagement across multiple organizations is to know what it looks like; the behaviors (not just attitudes) must be specified. Behaviors, to date, are the missing link in employee engagement. Thus, to fill that void, I suggest a role-based performance model as an option for providing a definition of the behaviors of employee engagement.

Role-Based Performance

The role-based performance model helps explain employee engagement by starting with the end goal in mind. The objective of all employee engagement initiatives is improved firm performance. The role-based performance model (see Figure 1) helps identify the types of behaviors needed from employees to drive performance. The model defines five key roles that employees occupy at work:

- Core job-holder role (what's in the job description)

- Entrepreneur or innovator role (improving process, coming up with new ideas, participating in others' innovations)

- Team member role (participating in teams, working with others in different jobs)

- Career role (learning, engaging in activities to improve personal skills and knowledge)

- Organizational member role (citizenship role or doing things that are good for the company)

I developed the role-based model for a large research project I conducted that focused on the determinants of long-term firm performance. The study was based on theories and prior work on what employers need from employees and what they reward. The model was

---

Firms win in the market when they develop human resources in a way that is not easily replicated.

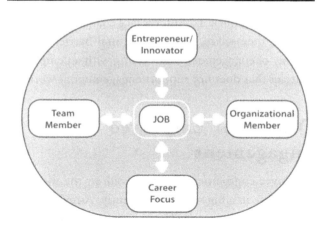

FIGURE 1. ROLE-BASED PERFORMANCE MODEL

validated with results obtained from numerous within-firm studies. The core ideas behind use of the model are that firms win in the market when they develop human resources in a way that is not easily replicated by their competition.

The roles that are not easily copied are the non-core job roles. When employees put in enough time within an organization to understand how to innovate (not just new products, but processes), they add value that an employee newly off the street cannot contribute. When employees are part of a team and all team members develop company-specific knowledge, that asset is something that cannot be easily copied by a competitor. As employees move from job to job within the organization and they build their own company-specific career knowledge, or as they teach others within the firm, the advantages of this firm-specific, career-based action cannot be easily imitated by another organization. When employees understand the inner workings of the organization, and they begin to engage in behaviors that support the company overall (instead of just their own job), this type of activity is not easily replicated by another organization, and these behaviors bring high value.

However, on the opposite side of the spectrum, if a company values only the core job role, and employees engage in behaviors exclusively associated with the core job, these jobs are very easy for competitors to copy. It is a simple matter to replicate this type of company,

Improving employee engagement calls for specifying the behaviors (not just the attitudes).

hire employees in another region or country who can be paid less money, and then compete with the original employer.

The net is that the core job role is important, but it alone will not result in long-term competitive advantage. This notion is consistent with what we are hearing in the employee engagement articles and books. Writers and experts talk about "above and beyond" behaviors, and they discuss discretionary effort, but these outcomes are rarely specifically defined or measured. Using the role-based model one can describe what it looks like to be engaged at work.

Employee engagement improves when employees are successful working in both the core job and the non-core job roles.

The result of employees engaging in the non-core job roles will be new ideas, improved process, enhanced product lines, more skilled employees, higher service levels, career movement within the organization, employees' going above and beyond to help the company even when a project is not officially part of the immediate job, employees working on teams to create new synergy that was not there in the past, employees caring about the outcomes of projects because they know that the organization values their going beyond their core job, and more. The result of spending time and doing the non-core job roles well is company-specific assets that cannot be easily copied. These assets, then, drive long-term competitive advantage and firm performance.

Leader Energy and Engagement

To provide the environment where employees can be successful in both the core job and the non-core job roles, a few things are necessary:

- Leaders themselves have to be engaged; they need to work and succeed in both their core job and non-core job roles.

- Leaders need to clearly articulate how each role helps support the business strategy and plan.

- Leaders have to create an environment where the non-core job roles are valued, and they must remove barriers to employees working in the non-core job roles.

These three conditions for engagement are not easy for leaders to meet. The work environment in most organizations is becoming more stressful, with employees not being able to do their core jobs in 60-hour work weeks, and leaders themselves are becoming burned out, confused, and disengaged. This is not a ripe environment for engaging employees or leaders.

Data on the context of engagement come from a study that I have been conducting over the last three years. The research is designed to examine leadership through an ongoing dialogue and data-collection process with leaders from multiple organizations. The study involves short pulse surveys sent every two months to more than 4,000 executives.

When leaders and managers are feeling distracted and overworked, their employees are doing much worse.

A subset of these data-collection efforts includes a measure of personal energy (or sense of urgency) at work, and the measurement process includes an open-ended comment question that asks respondents to explain the factors affecting their energy. The study focuses on energy because my prior research found it to be an important determinant of both individual and firm performance in several large-scale studies involving thousands of organizations and then in multiple case studies conducted since 1996.

The leadership pulse results show that, overall, leaders are reporting personal energy levels at work to be lower than where they say they are most productive. To understand this data, I asked respondents to explain their energy scores and why they are suboptimal. Below are some sample quotes from the data:

"Unclear and conflicting signals."

"Lack of information."

"Personnel problems."

"Non-recognition of extra effort—nobody appreciates."

"Stress, overwork, constantly changing priorities."

"Continuous crisis management and cost cutting moved energy level to both extremes."

"Too many projects; lack of completion."

"The feeling of overloading in the workplace."

"Today's pace is too fast, at home and at work, and it is difficult to stay ahead of the game."

In this study I obtained more than 250 single-spaced pages of comments that indicate that many senior executives are tired, struggling to keep pace with their workloads, unclear about their own priorities, not confident in their own business strategies, and overall not doing well. This leadership research is only the tip of the iceberg. When leaders and managers are feeling confused, distracted, and overworked, their employees are doing much worse. I have been collecting energy data from employees throughout the world since 1996. The research shows that a decline in leader energy predicts reduced employee energy scores.

Non-core job roles are what generate company-specific assets.

For example, here are sample quotes from a group of employees reporting to a manager whose own energy levels are suboptimal, low, and declining:

"Workload is not evenly distributed."

"Too much work and not enough time to get it done."

"The pace of my work is too much."

"I don't know how to spend my time; I have too much to do."

"I need help."

"There are not enough resources to get the job done."

"Many of us are just burned out."

"We have no idea what the strategy is or where we are going."

"There are not enough communications."

The Leader and Employee Engagement Challenge

This research suggests that many leaders are creating or are in an environment where employee engagement will be very difficult to achieve. When leaders are working at an energy level that is suboptimal, and when they have a difficult time merely getting their own jobs done, they will not value nor be interested in anyone engaging in the non-core job roles.

The type of environment leaders are discussing in the leadership pulse project is not conducive to high levels of employee or leader engagement. This is why having a concrete definition of what engagement looks like is so important for leaders. The organization must provide a context where people who move to the engaged state are rewarded or at least not punished for what they are doing. In a company where everyone is reporting being overworked, employees and managers will not tolerate time spent in the non-core job role even if a logical argument can be made for how that effort will benefit the organization in the long run.

In sum, the leadership pulse data reports a large proportion of leaders are not optimally energized at work, and the cause seems to be related to workload and a heavy focus on the core job role. At the same time, employees do not expect their employers to be loyal to them; they do not anticipate nor want jobs for life, and they are willing to leave their company when a new opportunity arises. In this highly complex environment, we need to ask some hard questions:

- Should anyone be surprised that only a small majority of employees are reporting being "engaged"? The employee contract was changed in ways that mean employers should have anticipated disengagement.

- Can anyone realistically expect to raise "engagement" when there are no associated rewards?

- Should we expect to improve engagement (if we define it as doing the non-core job roles) if employees are working for leaders who are having problems energizing themselves at work?

- Can employees or leaders afford to take time away from the job role when there are so many pressures on merely getting the job done?

A systematic approach to employee engagement begins with the leadership team.

The millions of dollars being spent on employee engagement programs may be wasted money.

- If the leadership team has no time to engage in anything other than the core job role, why would they value non-core job role-based behavior from their own employees?

Putting the pieces together, one could speculate that the millions of dollars being spent on employee engagement programs may be wasted money when the context for engagement does not exist. To change firm performance through people, a significant effort must begin with the leadership team. The leadership team must be engaged themselves; they need to know what it looks like to engage people at work, and they must be role models for this behavior with their direct reports—who then do the same for their employees.

Suggestions for Success

Improving conditions for employees and leaders at work so that they can engage in both core job and non-core job roles is an important goal for firms that want to gain competitive advantage. The role-based model is a way to start systematically addressing the problem of performance and the proposed solution of engagement.

If we define "engaged" employees as those who work and succeed in the non-core job roles, then a systematic approach to employee engagement would not start with an all-employee attitude survey (as has been done in many engagement programs). Instead, it would begin with the leadership team. Here are some suggested actions leaders can take to ensure that the people in charge of engagement are engaged themselves and that their organization has an environment that can support employees contributing to productivity in a way that is defined by the role-based model:

- Conduct a business analysis to determine what roles are really valued in their organization and what roles are needed to achieve business plan objectives. This analysis should lead to identification of any gap in shared understanding of how employees should be allocating time and effort and what is rewarded in the organization.

- If the non-core job roles are not valued (by the managers who interact with employees daily), analyze the types of structural and strategic changes required to align the organization so it can compete effectively.

- Determine what leadership education is necessary to create a culture where both core job and non-core job roles are valued and rewarded.

- Examine in detail what structural impediments may exist to spending time in the non-core roles. These can be formal processes such as performance management systems that only focus on the job, or they can be informal norms.

- Assess the ways in which the various roles need to be enacted throughout the year. The importance of roles may change based on seasonality of the industry or work demands; they also may be different for various occupations. This type of detailed understanding is needed to assure continuous alignment.

- Engage employees in the right roles at the right time. Conduct assessments to understand the determinants of engagement in the various roles as opposed to engagement overall. Using this data, you can develop interventions to help retain employees who are interested in engaging in both the core job and non-core job roles.

Organizations need more engagement at work. They need leaders, managers, supervisors, and employees who will take time to go above their core job roles if the business is to remain competitive in the global economy. However, employers cannot expect a magic formula to make engagement happen. It will be a long journey that starts at the top of the organization and moves its way throughout the business.

Theresa M. Welbourne is the founder, president, and CEO of eePulse, Inc., a technology and leadership research organization, as well as an adjunct professor of executive education at the Ross School of Business at the University of Michigan. She has more than 25 years' experience conducting research, teaching, consulting, and writing on the topic of leadership in high-growth and high-change organizations. She is also the editor-in-chief of Human Resource Management. Visit www.eepulse.com.

10 QUESTIONS TO STELLAR COMMUNICATION

Dianna Booher

Communication makes the "top three" in many lists today. The most important ingredient in happy marriages. The most essential element in raising well-adjusted teens. The most vital skill in job-interviewing success. The greatest problem voiced by political parties in gaining support for their candidate. The most frequent reason top talent joins a new team. The most critical component of great customer service. The biggest challenge leaders experience in times of change and upheaval.

It's all about communication. And success in business is all about how well you communicate—to your coworkers and customers.

Managers Inform; Leaders Connect

According to the late Peter Drucker, writing in the *Harvard Business Review* and summarizing his 65-year consulting career with CEOs, one of the eight key te-

nets of effective executives is taking responsibility for communication. Leaders lead; they take responsibility for the communication culture. Managers maintain; they go with the status quo.

Leaders become the face or human connection of an organization. They "connect" with other people—coworkers, clients, partners, each other—to get things done. Specifically, they communicate values. They act consistently with those values. They communicate respect and concern. They tell the truth.

What's the payoff personally in learning to be an exceptional communicator? You'll be able to

- Identify what to communicate, when to communicate it, and how to say it so that it sticks.

- Create compelling conversations to influence others to act.

- Connect with people to increase trust and cooperation.

Reprinted from Leader to Leader Number 46, Fall 2007

Effective leaders take responsibility for the communication culture.

- Facilitate understanding in complex, controversial, and difficult situations.

- Encourage information sharing rather than information hoarding.

- Build morale, improve team chemistry, and make others feel part of the group.

- Increase your credibility and impact when speaking before a group.

- Make others' work meaningful to them.

- Be able to coach others to improve their performance.

But hold on a moment before starting to sing "Kumbaya." You're not going to accomplish this miracle overnight—without answering the next question.

What do people—your boss, your cube mate, your kids—mean by the comment, "There's just no communication around here!" What makes people utter this complaint so frequently?

Why do people keep sending data, graphs, slides, and e-mail, thinking they're communicating? Why do parents keep talking "till they're blue in the face" and never get their kids to tune in? The answer to these questions just may be right under your own nose . . . literally.

Symptoms of Poor Personal Communication

Have you ever heard anyone say, "I'm a lousy communicator"? Hardly ever, I'll wager. The overwhelming majority of all résumés say "excellent oral and written communication skills." Most of us think we're great communicators. Unfortunately, our own understanding or response is not the best measure of effectiveness. Everything we say is clear to us—or we wouldn't have said it that way. So when we look *outward* for clues of poor communication, these symptoms often surface:

- Feeling that everyone agrees with and supports what you say, feel, and do most of the time

- Lack of input, questions, or feedback on your ideas presented in meetings

- Few or no ideas contributed in your meetings

- Inability to influence others to accept your ideas or change their viewpoint or behavior

- Seeing little or no behavioral change in people you've coached for improved performance

- Confusion about what you're supposed to be doing

- No understanding of the "why" behind assigned projects and goals

- Thinking that what you do or say doesn't really "change things" in the long run

- Nervousness or hesitancy about presenting new ideas to your boss, client, or strategic partners

- Ongoing conflict with peers or family

- Frequent rework

- Constant reminders from you to others to take action, meet deadlines, or send information

- Frequent requests for more information about topics or issues that you think you've already addressed sufficiently

- Feeling of disconnection and discomfort in one-to-one and small-group interactions

- Lack of positive feedback about your presentations or documents (from those not obligated to give it)

So for a more objective snapshot of your own skills when you're trying to keep from drowning in today's information deluge, ask yourself these ten questions about how well you communicate:

Is Your Communication Correct?

Lying at work, often gently referred to as *spin,* drains us and enrages us. The truth, the whole truth, and nothing but the truth . . . should not be three different things. And yet, spin drives our businesses and our lives. The challenge becomes to maintain truth and avoid lies without getting dizzy.

How do you regain trust in an environment where truth is hard to come by?

Nothing makes people believe you when you're right like admitting when you're wrong. Nothing earns more respect than confidently owning up to your own blunders, decisions, or poor performance—without denial or excuses. Ask a few has-been politicians, rock stars, or pro athletes how far denials took them in their pursuit of forgiveness after a major mess-up. Typically, the cover-up created more nasty noise and clutter in the media than the original offense. Likewise, in the workplace, there's tremendous power in being known as a person who tells the truth. Straight. Unvarnished. Direct.

Is Your Communication Complete?

Leaders often get so busy analyzing, problem solving, questioning, coordinating, deciding, and delegating that

To make people believe you when you're right, admit it when you're wrong.

they fail to communicate what's going on behind the scenes. Then they're puzzled when those who haven't been involved in the process don't readily buy in when they announce decisions and plans. You may recognize some of these attitudes, which all cause leaders to skimp on the details and leave others lagging behind.

Leave-the-Thinking-to-Us Mentality

Some leaders have a paternalistic culture. They view run-of-the-mill employees as the children of the organization, not to be trusted with the real facts, information, and explanations about decisions or actions.

Too Busy to Make Things Easier

Some people claim they're too busy to communicate. Consequently, they waste time in cleaning up the mess of miscommunication—settling conflicts, clarifying misunderstood missions, rewriting unclear documents, rehashing the same old issues in unproductive meetings, and shuffling misplaced priorities and missed deadlines caused by unclear directions.

Fear of Giving Bad News and Handling Negative Reactions

Let's face it: nobody likes to be the bearer of bad news. Fear leads to delay in telling bad news—even when the consequences threaten to engulf people. Positive people keep thinking, "If I put news of this impending problem off long enough, maybe I can solve things on my own—or at least mitigate the damage before I report it." The less complete information they share "in the interim," they think, the more opportunity to save the sinking ship. The only problem with that philosophy, of course, is that if their efforts prove unsuccessful, their full disclosure and warning come far too late; the damage is catastrophic.

So what's the antidote to the confusion and distrust caused by incomplete information? Consider the following new attitudes and actions:

- *Explain the reasoning behind your decisions.* You can't expect buy-in if people haven't traveled the same information road you've been driving.

What's the antidote to the confusion and distrust caused by incomplete information?

- *Focus on the how, not just the what.* Unless you're running for the Oval Office, tell people how you plan to implement things.

- *Be relevant rather than resented.* Interpret and translate the relevant details to the different people or groups involved.

- *Don't hide behind the technology.* What takes 10 e-mail messages to negotiate or clarify can often be communicated in a three-minute phone conversation. Pick up the phone—or walk down the hall to the next cubicle occasionally.

- *Communicate like you brush your teeth.* Make it a habit. Do it frequently, habitually, systematically. Get a system, a channel, a structure, a timetable that works for you. Informal chats in the hallway. Fireside chats in the lobby. Factory visits by the big cheese. Morning meetings between shifts.

Is Your Communication Clear?

We all assume we're clear when we write or speak. But just to make sure, we have a habit of tacking on the meaningless, "Any questions?" And when there are none, the tendency is to walk away from the conversation, assuming everyone got the message. Often, just the opposite is true. No questions may mean several things: People didn't understand enough of what you said to ask questions. They didn't understand the relevancy of your information to their job or plans. They

didn't understand they were supposed to take action based on your message.

Unexpected responses, blank stares, lack of coordination, and frequent rework are other signs that you may not be getting through.

So what to do?

- *Start with the punch line.* Whether delivering a presentation, writing e-mail, or briefing somebody in the hallway, make the opening line your punch line.

- *Be specific.* Never hide behind the old argument, "Oh, we're just arguing about semantics here." Words mean something. And therein lies the problem. Selection is central to understanding and agreement.

- *Make sure your nonverbal cues don't contradict your words.* Tell nonperformers that their behavior is unacceptable, but smile and nod encouragement at the wrong time during your discussion, and they may walk out thinking "no big deal" and revert to the status quo.

- *Adapt your style to the person and purpose.* Some people primarily take in information visually. Others pay attention to what they hear and rarely notice what they see. Still others learn and draw conclusions kinesthetically—primarily through what they experience through their own senses.

Is Your Communication Purposefully Unclear?

Indirect communication makes social camaraderie possible. If someone asks, "What do you think of my new office?" you don't typically respond, "It looks cheap. And if I had to look at this color of wall paint all day, I'd puke." Tact is the order of the day, and it makes life easier. But when it comes to discussions about problems and performance, direct discussion produces honest evaluation of issues and improves bad situations.

If you're the speaker, eliminate euphemisms that preclude meaning or action. Put yourself on the listening end of the message you just delivered: What comes to mind? If you draw a blank about your next action, not good. No matter the difficulty of your message, say it. If you want action, state it.

Is Your Communication Consistent?

Do your actions, policies, priorities, and practices match your words?

You communicate by what you reward and what you choose not to reward. You communicate by what you fund and what you don't fund. You communicate by what training you offer and what training you decide not to offer. You communicate by which policies you enforce and which you fail to enforce. You communicate by how many approval signatures you require on funding requests and the authorization limits on those approvals.

Credible communicators follow through with what they promise—or stop promising.

Are You as a Person Credible?

Generally, five things either contribute to or detract from people's inclination to believe you:

- *The Look:* Your appearance and physical presence, in dress, grooming, and body language.

- *The Language:* The words you choose and how well you think on your feet to express yourself.

- *The Likeability Factor:* Your personality and the chemistry you create between yourself and others: authenticity, vulnerability, approachability, a sense of humor, respect, courtesy—these are the traits that typically attract others and open their hearts and minds.

- *Character:* Your values and integrity.

- *Competence:* Your skill and track record of results.

If your message isn't sinking in . . . if you're not getting the action you want . . . maybe you should take it, well . . . personally.

Are You Concerned and Connected?

Leaders who show they care about people as individuals—not as employees, suppliers, or customers—make a connection. They engage—rather than just report the news. They consider the impact of the message they're delivering and are emotionally present. Likewise, they phrase sensitive news carefully rather than just blurt it out in meetings.

A big part of connection is listening as if you care. The following are *not* empathetic comments—no matter how many times you've heard them around the water cooler:

- "It could be worse."

- "Looks like you'll just have to tough it out."

- "You think *you've* got it bad—you should hear what we went through last year."

- "This may be a blessing in disguise."

Listening means focusing on the other person with sincere, not just polite, interest—and not just waiting your turn to talk.

Finally, connection involves acknowledging mistakes, shortcomings, and blame when necessary, and apologizing sincerely. It's a cold heart that cannot accept a sincere apology offered in true humility.

These are the ingredients of an apology that connects with people:

If your message isn't sinking in, maybe you should take it, well, personally.

- Admission of error, guilt, or wrongdoing. The person accepts responsibility for what was said or done and its inappropriateness, inaccuracy, weakness, hurtfulness, insensitivity, or whatever.

- Specificity. Apologizing specifically sounds sincere. Global, blanket apologies convey lack of concern or understanding of the situation or damage caused.

- Amends. Apologizing typically involves some attempt to make things right, some words or gesture of goodwill toward the offended person or group.

Is Your Communication Current?

Speed is the new measure of quality communication. If people typically receive your information only "the morning after"—the morning *after* they were supposed to have attended a meeting, the week *after* they were supposed to have submitted a report, the day *after* they were supposed to have been on a teleconference—consider why. Are you overwhelmed with the job and can't keep up with the workload? Are you not delegating tasks appropriately? Do you have an attitude of unresponsiveness? Do you fear giving negative news for fear of reaction?

Your answers to the previous questions are less relevant than the impression left with others waiting for responses. Those will be the questions forming in other people's minds when your information and responses always arrive "after the fact" or after they have already received "the news" from other sources.

So when faced with a time crunch, make it a habit to get information out today even in less-than-perfect form rather than wait until tomorrow for polished prose. Send information at the point of relevance—or not at all. In short, prefer substance over shine.

Does Your Communication Make You Look Competent?

People can't always follow you around to watch you fire a rocket, manage a research team, handle stubborn suppliers, or correct product-design flaws. But they do hear what you *say* or see what you *write* about that work. And they often judge your competence by what you communicate about your job—not necessarily by what they see firsthand.

Make Your Facts Tell a Story

The only thing worse than filling up your speech, slides, e-mail, or reports with fact after fact after fact . . . is not shaping them to tell your story. What story do your facts tell? What trail do the facts leave?

Use a Natural Delivery Style

My first challenge in coaching executives on their presentation skills is to bring their split personalities together—to help them learn to be their natural rather than unnatural self when speaking to a group. But remember that natural is not laid-back, winging it, unprepared, low energy, and monotone. Be your best, most natural self.

Make Your Bottom Line Your Opening Line

Forget the oral book report. Never fall prey to thinking, "I need to give them a little background first." Wrong approach. They'll never understand your background until they know your point. Instead, start with a summary of your key message. Then support your point with reasons, data, statistics, or whatever is necessary to tell your story and make the listeners or readers come around to your way of thinking and take action.

Be Passionate

Take your personality with you when you present your ideas to a group or enter the conference room for a meeting. Sometimes people insist that they're afraid to be *too* anything—too over the top, too strong, too overstated, too sold on the idea, too much the cheerleader. So in their quest not to be *too* anything, they lag in the land of *not very*—not very clear, not very sold on, not very eager, not very aggressive, not very enthusiastic, not very convinced, not very sure, not very prepared.

How passionate would you want your lawyer to be if pleading the facts of your insurance case to the jury? How passionate would you want your congressional representative to be when arguing for research funding for your medical condition? How passionate would you be in persuading investors to fund your new entrepreneurial venture? How passionate would you be about pleading with a kidnapper to release your child?

Passion rises and falls based on what's at stake. Your audience understands that concept all too well. They take their cues from you. Your interest interests them. The difference between *too* and *not very* can mean the difference between the life or death of your ideas and proposals.

Is Your Communication Circular?

Circular communication goes in all directions—or at least it should. That is, information and ideas should flow up the chain of command. Down the chain of command. Across departmental lines. From the day shift to the night shift. For the most part, such communication doesn't happen. At least, not routinely. How can you be a part of repairing this kink in the communication chain?

Cultivate Compelling Conversations

Think how often you replay conversations in your head—what you've said or plan to say to someone. Consider conversations a learning tool. They teach you both intellectual and emotional truth. That said, be the instigator of inspiring, intriguing conversations.

Know When to See the Whites of Their Eyes

As you encourage information exchange at all levels, you'll need to make a critical decision often. What's the best way to pass on this specific information? E-mail? Phone? Or a face-to-face conversation? A formal letter or report? The method you choose can make a tremendous difference in the results or action generated.

Learn to Connect All Along the Food Chain

In a culture that encourages conversations at all levels, you may find yourself talking with everyone from the CEO to the chauffeur. Be ready to connect at *their* point of interest.

Put "improved communication" in one of the top three slots on your own personal development plan this year. Stellar communication is the signature of star performers.

Dianna Booher is the author of "The Voice of Authority: 10 Communication Strategies Every Leader Needs to Know," from which this article is adapted. Author of more than 40 books, she is CEO of Booher Consultants, a communication training firm offering programs in oral presentations, writing, and interpersonal skills. She has been named one of the "21 Top Speakers for the 21st Century" by Successful Meetings magazine and has been featured in the New York Times, the Wall Street Journal, USA Today, and other publications. Find out more at www.booher.com.

THE
INFLUENTIAL
LEADER

Jack Stahl

Early in my career, I learned a key lesson in communication in a one-to-one conversation with a senior executive at Coca-Cola. I was trying to convince him to focus more energy on improving the quality of the financial controls inside one international business division. Initially, I centered my conversation on the problem—the breakdowns in controls and the lack of quality financial information coming from his operation. The executive got angry, and I realized I had offended him. The rest of our conversation was unproductive.

I decided to pull back. About a week later, after speaking to this executive's coworkers, I decided to take another approach. This time, I began our discussion by pointing out how he had succeeded with his division because he was an effective decision maker. I emphasized that I recognized that his influence had dramatically strengthened the operations for which he was responsible. After I recognized his importance to the company and his value as an individual, he relaxed.

Then I pointed out that perhaps we could improve the amount of information that he had available to him about his organization's operational performance. He seemed interested. Therefore, I suggested that having more information—the kind that required stronger

information and control systems—would help him make even better and faster decisions. By then he was paying close attention, even nodding in agreement. He understood that improving these systems would be win-win for the company and for him.

By working to connect with him—and by understanding and acknowledging his skills and strengths as a leader—I was able to offer a scenario that appealed to him and that he would support.

A Critical Key to Successful Leadership

The ability to influence others is fundamental to the success of all managers, executives, businesses, and organizations—just as it was to my own growth at Coca-Cola and then at Revlon. I worked at Coca-Cola from 1979 until 2001. During that time, I was fortunate to be afforded a clear vision of what was required to succeed at Coca-Cola, and I was coached by some remarkable leaders. Particularly from mentors like the late CEO Roberto Goizueta and former CEO Doug Ivester, I received the lessons, feedback, and advice that developed the core skills that I believe enabled me to be a successful leader.

   Reprinted from Leader to Leader Number 46, Fall 2007

These mentors made me aware of areas that I needed to develop and pointed out my mistakes as they encouraged the growth of my skills. Along the way, and ultimately as president of the company, I had a rare opportunity to play a role in Coca-Cola's ongoing success.

As gratifying as Coke's success was, it was also fulfilling to work for almost five years at Revlon, a company, like Coca-Cola, known for its wonderful brands. My time as CEO of Revlon offered me and my outstanding leadership team the opportunity to strengthen the strategies and capabilities of the company so that the company's marketplace and financial results would fully match the longtime strength and appeal of its brands.

I learned many leadership lessons from my experiences at these two great companies—and I describe them in detail in *Lessons on Leadership: The 7 Fundamental Management Skills for Leaders at All Levels.* In this article, however, I want to focus on what I think is a critical key to effective leadership: the ability to influence people.

Leaders obviously use many different types of communication to influence people. I use a mix of them—such as one-to-one contact, being visible and accessible, large group presentations, small group meetings, talking to people in hallways and elevators, e-mail, phone calls, faxes, written letters, newsletters, and memos. Whatever communication tools you use, I believe that effective communication and influence require understanding that as people consider or evaluate ideas, proposals, and presentations, they will make their decisions based on two key factors: the *merits* of proposals and ideas themselves, and their very human need to be *valued* as individuals.

Thus influencing people involves three broad components, or keys:

- Understanding your audience

- Building a connection between you and your audience

- Presenting your content effectively in real time

When you focus on these areas before, during, and after key communications, your impact as a leader will increase dramatically. After a while, you'll find yourself employing these practices naturally, and your preparation time will become less and less.

Understand Your Audience

Are you aware of the perceptions of your audience? Those perceptions or preconceived notions are your audience's *reality!* Try to understand them so you'll have the opportunity to shape your communication to change those perceptions.

While I was at Revlon, we interviewed candidates for senior leadership positions. At the start of an interview, I would often ask questions to help me understand the candidate's existing perceptions of Revlon. Sometimes the interviewees would raise concerns about the credibility of the company and our perceived lack of financial resources. Once I understood their negative perceptions, I was able to demonstrate that we were building a capable leadership team and assured them that we would indeed have access to financial resources to generate growth for our business. When you address their concerns and perceptions up front, you allow your audience to be more relaxed and feel comfortable that you understand their needs and will respond to them.

Here are some questions to ask yourself about how actively you try to understand your audience:

When you make a presentation before a group, are you arriving well before your presentation starts, talking to people likely to be members of your audience, and asking questions that will help you understand their perceptions, goals, strategies, and challenges? Arriving at a presentation early can be a good opportunity to gain insight into the minds of your audience members. It's also helpful to get input from other people who understand your audience.

Are you staying late after presentations? This gives you a chance to debrief your audience—to obtain feedback that will tell you whether you were successful in communicating your message. This is an important part of understanding your audience and shaping subsequent communication. At Revlon, we held monthly operating reviews typically attended by 25 to 30 people to consider every part of our North American business. After one operating review of a major new product initiative for the Almay brand, members of our leadership team informally asked other attendees for feedback. Several people at the meeting were concerned that the project involved developing and producing hundreds of new SKUs (stock-keeping units) in one year, which was operationally complex and would require tremendous communication across all functions of the company. This was a valid concern. Revlon leaders then formed a new routine involving key people responsible for managing the project. They would hold a detailed weekly meeting and discuss every element of the Almay brand new product initiative. This small change, brought about by taking the time after a meeting to listen for concerns, increased confidence in the initiative and enabled its successful execution.

Are you aware of who in your audience are the "broadcast towers"? Broadcast towers are people who *carry significant influence* with the remainder of your audience. These people can be either your biggest supporters or your biggest detractors. By knowing and understanding who they are in advance, you can choose how much time and energy to spend trying to influence them.

When I was president of Coca-Cola North America, I realized that a few small Coca-Cola bottlers carried disproportionate influence with the other 86 bottlers, most of which were much larger companies. I spent a lot of time working to understand—and address—the concerns of these smaller bottlers so that they could become a positive influence on the rest.

Take the time after a meeting to listen for concerns.

Cynics often ask questions important to others.

Are you thoroughly addressing the questions of the most analytical (and sometimes seemingly cynical) members of your audience? In most audiences, there will be at least one cynic, but these people often ask discerning questions that are important to others who may have questions lurking in their minds that they were afraid to ask publicly.

I have seen many senior leaders be dismissive of a tough, analytical questioner and turn off an entire audience. Treat these questions and the questioners with the respect they deserve. These situations can create opportunity to influence an audience. Your answers and the tone you use in responding to the questions may be the key to how the majority in the room evaluates you and whether they open their minds to your ideas. A certain amount of group identification psychology is present in every audience and must be recognized and respected.

Do you recognize that people communicate in different ways? Does an individual you are trying to influence require facts and data to relate to your idea, or is this someone with whom you need to discuss an issue on a more conceptual (or even emotional) level? When dealing one to one, try to be sensitive to how people prefer to be influenced. It will make you a more effective communicator with each person.

Initially, one of my direct reports and I had a difficult time communicating. Finally, I appealed to a communications consultant to evaluate our problem. After some observation, the consultant pointed out that this individual preferred a lot of facts and data—information was the key to opening a line of communication. I began focusing my discussions with her on facts and analysis, rather than concepts or strategy. As a result of coming to comprehend *her* way of thinking, my ability to communicate positively with her improved dramatically.

Demonstrating from the outset that you *understand* who the audience is will help the audience to focus on *the rest of your message.* I often found that in one-to-one conversations, if I began by acknowledging the skills or strengths of the individual, the conversation was likely to be more relaxed and productive. Try discussing experiences you've both shared in the past or common problems.

Build a Connection Between You and Your Audience

The people you are trying to influence do not want to be held to a standard of perfection; that is impossible. Lead with humility. For you and your audience to relate and connect, they need to know that you do not expect them to be perfect. The best way to do that is to let them know that you are aware of your own limitations. That sense of humility and vulnerability develops a sense of openness with your audience that leads to successful communication. People will be more readily influenced by someone who doesn't pretend to be perfect, who is humble, and doesn't expect perfection from them.

To establish a connection with your audience, you need to self-disclose, even overdisclose. Take some risk in terms of how much you disclose about your thoughts, feelings, and the reasons behind your thinking. People will better connect to your ideas and to you as a leader. My own experience suggests that demonstrating trust invites the same from your listeners.

Humor and passion are important communication tools and can help reveal your personality. Humor can

Let people know that you are aware of your own limitations.

People want events that are important to them to be important to you.

be an excellent way of breaking tension and helping to get across a complicated idea, as can a sense of passion or commitment. Show people that you really care about an idea, and they will be more likely to think it's important. At Revlon, we had an annual North American sales conference where the marketing department showed new marketing plans. Rather than make their presentations in the traditional format, one year they created a mock news broadcast announcing the marketing news for the upcoming year. The presenters showed sides of their personalities that were not only very funny but also demonstrated their enthusiasm for their ideas. These presentations were very effective in energizing the sales force.

Show up for key events and important milestones. People want events that are important to *them* to be important to *you.* For example, you should understand whether it would be meaningful to your customers for you to attend conferences, trade shows, and conventions that they host. Though it's expensive, sometimes traveling a long distance to attend a customer's key event can send a strong message about how much you value that customer.

Make sure you are publicly giving people credit for their accomplishments. This seems obvious, but you can sometimes "value" the whole group when people hear others receiving credit for good work. For example, as I mentioned earlier, Revlon held routine meetings with our employees to update our people on the company's progress. Then we switched to letting employees be the main speakers at these meetings. It was a very positive experience for the employees to learn that management appreciated them and their efforts to develop new ideas and solutions to move the business forward. Whenever we had a chance to recognize by name an individual who had created success, we looked for ways to do it during these employee conferences. It created tremendous goodwill. It also encouraged other people to find ways to move the business forward even faster.

Be careful to avoid publicly embarrassing people when finding a mistake or problem. Working to understand the *underlying systemic reason* for a problem so that changes can be made to how work gets done is very important. In this situation, it can be worthwhile to call out significant lessons from that breakdown publicly in order to avoid repeating it. Yet if the mistake occurred due to a skill gap or deficiency in a particular person, my experience is that the first discussion should be with that person privately. One-to-one communication will probably be more successful in motivating the individual to improve needed skills. Publicly embarrassing someone often makes that person (and others around) withdraw, and prevents them from taking more effective action in the future. When I made the mistake of publicly embarrassing someone, I often found that it took significant time for me to repair the damage I had done.

Present Your Content Effectively in Real Time

The best presenters show flexibility and have the ability to react in the moment. This requires focusing on the audience and observing how they are responding to your communication. You should look for reactions from your audience—facial expressions, body language—that signal confusion or misunderstanding. If you see this, move to clarify or reinforce an important point. If you see reactions like disinterest, sleepiness, or covert use of BlackBerrys, it may signal that it's time to take a break, sum up, or regroup. If an audience member seems to react negatively to one of your key points, you may need to find an opportunity to readdress that point later in your remarks, or after the presentation in a question-and-answer period.

The ability to think on your feet comes in part from *overpreparation on the basics* of your presentation be-

forehand. Often, early in my career, my colleagues kidded me about always seeming to overrehearse for presentations. I did that because I was taught that by being well versed in the basic content materials, you can employ your energy to *focus on your audience*, rather than worry about the specifics of your remarks. This helps you to be really responsive to your audience and adjust your prepared presentation based on what you are seeing or hearing. Overpreparing—allowing you the time, energy, and ability to react to the moment at hand as needed—can be an enormous help to the overall success of your presentation.

Are you allowing enough time for people to process what you have told them? People need time to embrace new ideas. Give them a chance to digest what you are communicating. In a small group or one-to-one dialogue, check people on their understanding by asking them questions that will get them to summarize what they have heard. This will also help cement their understanding of what you have said. During intense negotiations, once you have made a significant amount of progress and have "moved the ball" in a positive direction, suggest taking a break. This gives people time to solidify in their minds what has been agreed upon and refresh themselves before you move on.

Are you staying the course with your communication? It is very important to have conviction and be appropriately persistent about your ideas in order to communicate effectively.

At Revlon, our consistent message was that by focusing on our consumers, our customers, and our own organization, and by working to strengthen our business with these three constituencies, we could create tremendous success for our company. We constantly addressed exactly what we were doing to drive the business in these important areas. For example, our quarterly earnings announcements and our employee updates were always organized in this fashion.

We measured and communicated positive results against these three strategic building blocks; negative results were discussed in much the same way. Our communication was frequent and sometimes seemed repetitive. But we were always consistent in saying that

Your success depends on your ability to influence people—and your ability to listen to and be influenced by others.

focusing on these three areas would bring success. By doing so, we encouraged employees to focus their actions in these three areas.

Influencing Others Requires Listening to Them

As should be clear by now, communication is a two-way street. Your success as a leader depends on your ability to influence people—but it also depends upon your ability to listen to and be influenced by others to take the actions that will benefit your organization. Remember, it is essential that you spend time talking with people—not only to reinforce your key messages but also to listen to their concerns and challenges, and to provide feedback.

While I was at Revlon, we decided to recruit for several key marketing and sales positions. However, the company was having trouble attracting the kind of talent we were seeking. So one day I stopped by to see the head of our recruiting department. After this drop-in, I realized that I had not been paying enough attention to this critical function. I learned that we were significantly understaffed with recruiters to meet the challenge of hiring the number of marketing and salespeople we needed. At the same time, the recruiters that we had did not have adequate materials describing the company's progress to demonstrate to potential recruits that Revlon would be an excellent place to further their careers.

After this discussion, we added significant resources—and more leadership oversight—to our recruiting function, including materials describing our progress and opportunities for advancement at Revlon. This adjustment allowed us to attract additional employees of the caliber we desired. This is just one example of *taking the time to listen to the challenges of your people.* The truth is, you can't create organizational success alone.

Jack Stahl is the author of "Lessons on Leadership: The 7 Fundamental Management Skills for Leaders at All Levels," which has just been published. He joined The Coca-Cola Company in 1979 as a treasury analyst, served later as the company's chief financial officer and, after successfully leading the company's businesses in North America and Latin America, became president of The Coca-Cola Company. He was appointed president and CEO of Revlon in 2002 and led the company through a five-year period in which its market share, profitability, and balance sheet were strengthened. He currently serves on the boards of the Schering-Plough Corporation and The Boys & Girls Clubs of America and is chairman of the board of the United Negro College Fund.

MASTERING THE ART OF GIVING ADVICE

James E. Lukaszewski

D o you want to have influence? Most people would say, "Of course!" Having influence means being remembered and being in on decisions and strategy well before the strategies are selected and the decisions need to be made. Those with influence make an impact on their organizations and the larger world and can advance more rapidly in their careers.

Here's a test of your current level of influence in your organization. Do people hold up meetings, waiting for you to arrive to make important contributions or interpretations of current events? Do people remember what you say and perhaps quote you in other places and venues? Do people tell your stories and share your lessons as though those stories belong to them? Do people learn things from you that they acknowledge to you and remark about to others? Do others seek out your opinion and ideas or share their agendas and beliefs with you in the hope of influencing you to influence the behavior of others more senior than you?

Regardless of how you answer those questions, one of the realities of corporate life is that there is only so much face time, airtime, meeting time, and thinking time available to those who lead organizations. You can have influence only to the extent that people take time

out of their busy days to listen to you and pay attention to your advice. There is an art to giving advice, as I have discovered.

For more than 30 years, I have advised top executives facing issues ranging from media-initiated investigations to product recalls and plant closings, from ethics failures and criminal litigation to corporate takeovers and serious executive malfeasance. My job is always to help these individuals, and those they rely on, to recognize the nature of the times, and to adapt effectively to continue running organizations with championship, leadership, compassion, and accountability.

Over the years, I have learned a lot of lessons about working CEOs, boards, and senior executives, which I detail in my new book, *Why Should the Boss Listen to You? The Seven Disciplines of the Trusted Strategic Advisor.* In this article, I want to focus on the art of giving advice.

The Art of Giving Advice Effectively

Your advice may be perceptive, even wise, but if it falls on deaf ears, it helps no one. Beyond the actual quality of your advice, how you communicate that advice plays

   Reprinted from Leader to Leader Number 50, Fall 2008

Do people hold up meetings, waiting for you to arrive?

a major role in ensuring that others can and will listen to it and act on it. The six approaches suggested here can help achieve this goal.

Be Positive

In business conversation, when someone says something with which you disagree, you may be inclined to respond with something like, "You're wrong," or "That's incorrect," or "You don't know what you're talking about," or "It's simply not done that way," or some similar negative approach. You may then explain what is correct or how you really do things, but your listener is still dealing with the insult of your negative language. This makes it almost impossible to hear your constructive language. Negative comments almost always put others on the defensive even though we have important, positive, constructive things to say.

"The Bad News Eradicator" is an exercise I do with clients in which I present a list of common negative phrases and then turn them into positives. Here is a small sample of the negative-to-positive transformations:

Negative	Positive
"We don't do it that way."	"Here's the way we do it . . . "
"That's not our style."	"Here are important elements of our style . . . "
"The boss won't buy it."	"Here's what the boss has bought in the past; here's what we may be able to sell in the future . . . "
"That's a lie."	"If you check your facts and assumptions you may come to a different conclusion." Or, "Using the same analysis we came up with a different, more positive result."

The lesson is this: Your use of negative language needlessly obstructs and damages your relationship with other people. Eradicate or eliminate negative and emotional words and you become far more powerful and in control of almost any situation. Your positive approach blocks or defeats those who are negative. Most arguments, misunderstandings, confusion, and aggressive behavior are triggered by negative words, phrases, and attitudes. In situations of confrontation and controversy, at least one side of the argument needs the negativity of the other to continue operating effectively and pushing the argument forward. Eliminate that negative energy, and progress can actually be made, or a more peaceful resolution can be sought.

Eliminate Criticism as a Coaching and Advising Practice

As a teaching and change technique, criticism leads to very bad results. The people you advise are hurt or confused. Often negative advice leads to even more negative behavior. "Constructive criticism" is an oxymoron. Angry, negative language generates a future with angry, negative people. Positive outcomes require positive language.

Here's an example: Recently a friend called. She was in charge of evaluating the performance of the new minister in her church after a year's service. She put together a brief letter to members of the congregation asking that they provide some criticism. I believe she used the words "constructive criticism" of the minister's performance. She mailed 700 copies. She received more than 500 responses, each of which contained an average of three comments. Some contained even more.

As a teaching and change technique, criticism leads to very bad results.

The feedback was devastating. If you added up all the criticism, there was no way this minister could possibly continue in the job and survive emotionally. Most of the criticisms were negatives; many reflected individual misunderstandings, and virtually none reflected knowledge of the scope of the congregation's mission or the daily activities required of the minister as the congregation's leader. My friend's problem was, of course, that she had to share this information with the minister. If she didn't have something else worked out, he would undoubtedly resign. Even though the congregation really liked this man and wanted him to stay, even a minister could not withstand this level of personal criticism.

I told her about a lesson I learned early in my career from Chester Burger, now retired, who was one of America's most famous, beloved, and influential business communications consultants for many decades. Rather than criticizing past performance, his strategy, which I've followed for years, was to ask each client executive to make one positive and constructive suggestion about what that executive might do to achieve the goals of the organization. The application of this technique is incredibly powerful.

My friend did go back and use this technique. She wrote a simple note to congregation members asking them to suggest up to three things the pastor could do in the next six to nine months to move the congregation into the future. Out of the 700-member congregation, she received 12 suggestions. Each was implementable and achievable within a 30- to 90-day period. My friend went back to the minister, in all honesty, and showed the first assessment from the congregation, but then showed the follow-up work. The minister not only stayed, but implemented every suggestion in the first 90 days.

The lesson is this: We have the power to structure and control productive discussions and debate. If you want constructive results, seek and insist on constructive suggestions. You'll get very few, but what you get will be useful. If you are constructive and seek positive, constructive suggestions, you automatically control and therefore powerfully manage how decisions are made.

Speedy decisions and actions help you outrun those who love to live in the past.

Urge Prompt Action

Over the years I've learned that whether it's a group of activists, angry employees, upset neighbors, or jealous competitors who appear to be threatening, the way to win, the way to move things forward, the way to stay in charge is to act now, and do it now . . . every time.

Speedy decisions and actions help you outrun the competition and those who love to live in the past. The longer it takes a senior manager or senior leader to respond, the more complex solving the problem becomes. In this day and age, every leader, and certainly every trusted adviser, should be prepared for surprise to the point where they can avoid time-consuming meetings and delays by exercising preauthorized responses to attacks, problems, instability, fear, mistakes, or errors.

This often means making smaller decisions and acting on them more quickly. Some useful responses:

- *Answer it now.* If you face questions, get the answers and get them now.

- *Ask it now.* Rather than waiting for someone else to ask the serious question, ask first to get the answer.

- *Challenge it now.* If it's wrong, correct it. If it's legitimate, act on it. If it's an alternative worth considering, decide and act.

- *Act now.* If you know something is going to be a problem, work now to eliminate the cause.

- *Fix it now.* If it's broken, move to repair it; if it's breaking down, move to shore it up.

The lesson is this: Those who act promptly, who do it now, are ahead of the competition and produce fewer new critics, enemies, and naysayers. Prompt action often foils the opposition's most carefully laid plans, and can defeat almost any critic, while better controlling the situation.

Linear thinkers may criticize you for this, saying, "Move that fast and you'll make more mistakes." But mistakes will be made anyway. Deferring them to some other time only delays success and makes them worse. Make the inevitable mistakes early. Fix them faster and move on more successfully. You'll just make different mistakes earlier.

Focus on Outcomes

Always focus on a goal. In 1995, I was deeply involved in negotiations between some powerful anti-corporate forces: groups of labor unions, church groups, and nongovernmental organizations. The issues were extraordinarily compelling, in the news, divisive, and to some extent in the streets. The challenge was to find a way to sit down face to face, put these matters in some perspective, and develop a plan of action.

Fortunately, someone suggested that we meet with a minister in Brooklyn Heights, New York, just across the East River from Manhattan. He was reputed to have the personal presence and an unusual strategy for managing such a politically charged confrontation.

We met in his living room in December. This huge, jovial man greeted us warmly, asked us to sit down together in front of a roaring fire, listen to some music, and be quiet for a few minutes.

He then laid down just one ground rule for the day's work: the discussion was to be entirely outcome-focused. This meant that whatever happened between us prior to entering his living room was out of bounds (disagreements, arguments, behaviors, truth, fiction, and lies). The past was completely off limits to our current discussion. This was the fundamental ground rule. If this ground rule was a problem, he promised to end the discussions and bid us a pleasant day.

It's crucial to understand just how powerful this concept is. Fundamentally, it recognizes that everyone owns yesterday, last week, last month, and last year, from their own point of reference. That ownership is permanent. Even given a limitless amount of discussion, the past will remain as it was, owned by those who were there.

But no one owns the future—the next 15 minutes, the next day, the next week, the next month, the next year. Therefore, when we choose to be outcome-focused, we are choosing to enter, live, and build a future together.

Now back to Brooklyn Heights. Each time anyone began a discussion supported by something from the past, our host would halt the discussion and refocus it on tomorrow. It was tough for these real-time adversaries to stick to the process, but by 4:30 that afternoon we had negotiated and signed a one-page agreement containing just six sentences. That agreement was reached on December 15, 1995. Those who signed it, and the businesses and organizations they represented, still live by it today.

The lesson is this: Focus on tomorrow and only take from yesterday the positive, useful, constructive elements and ideas that can move the process forward, promptly. There will be very few, if any. Focusing on the future allows you to build tomorrow free of the problems, misunderstandings, and crippling assumptions of the past.

Bonus lesson: Applying this single concept will substantially cut meeting and discussion time. A good portion of most meetings is spent explaining to those who weren't at the last meeting what went on and what has yet to be done. Then, it's necessary to explain again because some of those who attended the last meeting have a very different perception of what went on than you do. What little time remains is finally used to get something done and move ahead. Skip yesterday; go straight to tomorrow and save tons of time.

No one owns the future.

You get to the future faster by starting there.

Tomorrow can only start when today is over. Todays that are governed by yesterday only cause more problems and may even prevent a successful tomorrow. Outcome focus saves precious time, reduces mistakes and misunderstandings, and acts as a positive force for moving ahead.

You get to the future faster by starting there.

Be an Incrementalist

An incrementalist strives for the successful forward step rather than the global solution. Most top leaders are skeptical of silver bullets, big ideas, and brilliant strategies. They realize that progress made incrementally, often following established patterns of thinking and experience, applied after rigorous exploration and study with a hint of intuition and strategic thinking, can actually trigger powerful insights. The incrementalist breaks problems into solvable parts and works to resolve each increment of the problem promptly.

Being an incrementalist actually prepares the leader and the organization to watch for and recognize big breakthroughs. Such breaks are as much a matter of luck as anything. Luck is limited. Luck actually comes most often to those who are relentlessly incremental in their personal progress every day. As Louis Pasteur so famously said, "Chance favors the prepared mind."

The most credible advisers are those who relentlessly and intentionally:

- Grow and learn every day.

- Help those they serve to achieve some positive incremental progress every single day.

- Identify and talk about those positive increments that they work with, supervise, or achieve every day.

- Assess daily what they've learned, and then teach those learnings to others.

Be Pragmatic

Your credibility rests more on what you are actually able to accomplish than on any series of goals or concepts you may choose to announce—but achieve only partially, or fail to achieve at all. Pragmatic advisers focus on what's doable.

One of the more interesting stories about pragmatism appears in Jack Welch's book, *Straight From the Gut.* He had just finished listening to nuclear engineers decide how they were going to begin selling three nuclear reactors per year in the United States, and how that would save this General Electric division.

After listening for an hour, Welch thoughtfully responded that no matter how good their intentions were, nuclear reactors were not going to be sold again in the United States in their lifetime, so they needed to focus on some other aspect of their business, perhaps servicing existing nuclear facilities. GE is now top in its category of servicing nuclear facilities. Mr. Welch was being a pragmatist.

The lesson is this: A pragmatist matches rhetoric with reality. Put yourself in the other person's shoes. See the world from their perspective. Enlist their help in achieving your goals by helping them achieve a portion of their goals in ways they recognize, and from their own perspective. Dale Carnegie was right: "Help the other guy get what he wants, from his perspective; and he'll help you get what you want, from your perspective."

Most top leaders are skeptical of silver bullets and brilliant strategies.

Be a Strategic Force

Giving advice effectively is a strategic force that helps drive individuals, organizations, cultures, and societies forward every day. One of the greatest frustrations of organizational life, especially for individuals aspiring to be influential, is not being invited to important meetings or being invited in too late. By the time you do get called in or become aware of what's going on, or are permitted to participate, all the expensive outside consultants, attorneys, and assorted advice givers have staked out all the avenues you might have successfully recommended. The discipline of being intentionally constructive, with a relentlessly positive approach, helps those you advise be more receptive to the help you offer. You will become influential. You'll get invited in earlier. Maybe they will even begin holding up meetings until you arrive.

James E. Lukaszewski is the author of "Why Should the Boss Listen to You? The Seven Disciplines of the Trusted Strategic Advisor." He is the founder, CEO, and chairman of The Lukaszewski Group, helping leaders and managers contain and counteract tough, touchy, and sensitive issues on a daily basis. Visit his Web site at www.e911.com.

PROMOTING THE HEALTHY FLOW OF INFORMATION TO SENIOR LEADERS

Ira Chaleff

We are often uncomfortable with the idea of being called a follower. We want to act as a leader and be recognized as a leader. And we want everyone who works for us to be a leader.

What's wrong with that picture? First, when we lead, don't we want those who report to us to follow? Second, if we report to a leader, doesn't that leader expect us to support his or her values, vision, and strategy? Isn't that following?

The obvious point is that sometimes we lead and sometimes we follow. These are roles we play and roles we expect others to play. And they both need to be played well.

The best followers behave very much like dance partners. What does it mean to play the follower role well?

Think of a dance. The leader doesn't want to drag a limp follower around the dance floor. Good dance partners exert a certain tension in moving with the leader. They stay alert for shifts a leader is about to make and prepare to synchronize with the new move. They detect missteps the leader makes and compensate for those as gracefully as possible. They compel the leader to give them sufficient attention to be able to partner well. They follow with strength.

In organizations, the best followers behave very much like dance partners in their relation with leaders. But there is an important difference. On the dance floor there may be many couples, but in most dances none of these exert authority over the others. Each leader and follower need only be aware enough to avoid colliding with the other couples, while staying focused on their own interactions.

 Reprinted from Leader to Leader Number 56, Spring 2010

In contrast, in large organizations, leader-follower pairs typically report to superior leader-follower pairs, forming hierarchical chains in which those who are leaders downward are followers upward. Now a terrific leader-follower partnership in the middle of the organization may be answering to a follower-leader partnership above in which the follower doesn't follow with strength or the leader doesn't lead with strength.

The choreography is coming from the top of this chain but those in between the strong partners at the bottom and top of the chain aren't being good conduits of information about conditions on the dance floor, the excitement or fatigue of the dancers, the quality of the music, or the engagement of the audience.

We tend to think that senior leaders are in the best position to remedy this situation. But remember, they don't have very good data on which to assess the situation, let alone to intervene and improve it. Those at the lower levels are in a much better position to observe and analyze the issues and generate ideas for remedying them.

A seismic shift has occurred in many organizations. The deepest knowledge in the organization no longer resides at its top echelons, it is embedded in the middle and bottom. The more that organizations become collections of knowledge workers, the more leaders are dependent on their followers to help them understand threats and opportunities that reside in continuously evolving technologies and emerging social and environmental trends.

The obvious point is that sometimes we lead and sometimes we follow.

You can preach all you want about candor.

What can the senior leaders do to ensure the organization gets the data and ideas from lower in the hierarchy to the higher levels? While those on lower rungs can take various initiatives to help the organization correct itself, ultimately they need support from senior levels. First let's briefly identify the barriers and then examine the potential remedies.

Barriers to the Upward Flow of Information and Ideas

Several barriers must be understood and overcome:

Processes That Distort Information

We're all familiar with the telephone game, the distortions in meaning that occur as messages are relayed along a chain, and its analogy to organizational communication. But we still discount its ability to dilute and distort information. While more organizations rely on omni-directional networks to process information, many decisions are still based on critical data that moves upward linearly in report form. What happens to the data at each level can preserve or dilute its power.

Senior leaders can digest just so much information. Thus the information that wends its way through multiple levels to the top of the hierarchy is condensed and recondensed. At each level, those who believe they know what their senior leaders want and don't want to hear will spin, scrub, summarize, and sanitize the reports. Approval processes designed for efficiency are used instead to manage image and perception.

Hierarchical Relationships

Even when personnel at lower ranks have the opportunity to report reality as they see it directly to senior leaders, cultural mechanisms can interfere with the process. Hierarchical structure clarifies who can commit the organization to large endeavors and their attendant costs, clearly a necessary function. But hierarchical relationships, or the unspoken rules in society of how to behave toward superiors and subordinates, can interrupt the transmission of important information and perspectives.

When constrained by the rules of hierarchical relationship, a follower may be at the table when a superior provides wrong information to the senior executive present and may refrain from correcting the information because of those unspoken rules. Unless greater value is placed on providing full and accurate information than on avoiding minor embarrassments between ranks, leaders can be misled into making poor decisions.

Organization Culture

Within the general societal rules governing relationships, each organization evolves its own culture. Leaders often inherit cultures that frown on too much candor. They cannot preach against this culture. It is entrenched and difficult to transform. They must demonstrate the desired new culture by their actions. Yet often the old culture serves to reinforce leaders' sense of prerogative. It is seductive for leaders to slip into the perks of that established culture. It requires a clear organizational philosophy to begin modeling the advantages of new ways of relating that better serve the organization.

Opening Channels of Communication

While courageous followers do not wait for leaders to make the environment safe for candor, here are ten

Leaders can be misled into making poor decisions.

ways that leaders can promulgate and support a culture of increased productive candor:

Encourage Self-Organizing Groups

Using the power of communications technology, staff from across all disciplines and locations can organize themselves into working groups to address organizational needs. When these spring up, support them! If the pump needs priming, encourage groups to form around these concerns. Ensure that whenever possible at least some of the groups' ideas are adopted and that those who contributed to the generation of those ideas are acknowledged. Be ferocious if needed to ensure the hierarchy doesn't sideline or quash these efforts.

Electronic MBWA

Traditional management philosophy encourages Management by Walking Around. In multinational organizations and very large agencies and conglomerates this strategy has practical limits. In the electronic communications age, however, it can be simulated by "dropping in" on electronic communications forums that organization staff or clients use to work through issues. Be a gracious visitor, applauding improvement efforts, respectfully asking questions to clarify concerns, and being of assistance where you can. Do nothing to inhibit the free flow of communication in these forums.

Model Multilevel Meetings

Be very mindful, when you are conducting meetings in which several levels of the hierarchy are present, that the unspoken rules of hierarchical relationship are probably operating. Stay alert for opportunities

Thoughtful, divergent views have an important place.

to disrupt these and model more open rules of relationship. Make use of a rotating "Devil's Advocate" role and acknowledge those who play the role most courageously and productively.

Capture Teachable Moments

You can preach all you want about candor, but until the group sees your responses to candor people will remain cautious. Notice and applaud instances of courageous candor or dissent. Explain why you found the instance valuable. Stay alert for weak signals and mitigating language that tells you there is more to the concern than the individual is expressing. Encourage tentative voices to elaborate so you fully understand potential problems before moving on to other matters.

Institute Minority Reports

Don't let dissident voices be marginalized. Let the hierarchy fashion the report it feels serves you best but insist that minority reports also make their way to you. Frown on attempts to discourage these. Set standards for length so they are manageable, but disallow content editing. The majority can attach a rebuttal of similar length but may not pressure the dissenting voices to mute their concerns.

Create Skip-Channel Norms

Managers who report to you will, with little hesitation, say that if staff two or more levels below them are troubled by actions of their direct supervisors, they can always talk to that manager directly. These same managers will often express consternation if a lower-level report goes above their head to you. Convene a conversation to identify any barriers to skipping channels in the rare situations in which doing so seems important or necessary. Help the group establish norms for skip-channel communication with which everyone can live.

Give Awards for Courageous Dissent

Periodically give out awards for courageous dissent. Choose examples in which the way the dissent to senior leadership was expressed was both courageous and productive. Make service to the mission more valuable than conformance to hierarchical orthodoxy. Make it clear that between the extremes of rote compliance and counterproductive undermining of lead-

Encourage tentative voices to elaborate so you fully understand potential problems.

ership, there is an important place for thoughtful, divergent views.

Hold Followers Accountable

Set up norms that hold followers accountable for conveying concerns to leadership. Be clear that telling the leadership once about a concern and then washing one's hands of it if leadership doesn't immediately respond is not valued behavior. If leaders fail to grasp the importance of the concern being raised, followers are accountable for doing a better job of documenting and conveying their concerns before giving up the effort.

Be Aware of Your Own Biases

Leaders often have a bias toward seizing opportunities rather than heeding warnings of risk. Sometimes this bias is reversed and leaders are so risk averse they hesitate to pursue opportunities followers have identified. "Know thyself" is once again central. If you tend to minimize risk, discipline yourself to pay more attention to followers' efforts to alert you to significant risk. If you tend to place too much attention on risk, discipline yourself to utilize the organization's machinery to more objectively assess the risk-reward ratio.

Develop Both Your Leaders and Your Followers

Remember that the cultural, psychological, and organizational barriers to candor are powerful. Engage the power of targeted training to develop new language, mental frames, strategies, and skills to support making productive candor a norm in both the leader and follower roles.

As long as hierarchies are with us, leaders should pay close attention to how they affect good data and candid views reaching them. Take every opportunity to make greater use of networks and egalitarian communication technologies to reduce the negative effects of hierarchy. But recognize that hierarchy is still present and encourage steps to soften its impact on the candor all senior leaders need.

Ira Chaleff is president of Executive Coaching and Consulting Associates (www.exe-coach.com) and author of "The Courageous Follower: Standing Up To and For Our Leaders," which is now in its third edition. He was named one of the 100 best thinkers on leadership by Leadership Excellence and is the founder of the International Leadership Association's Followership Learning Community. Visit www.courageousfollower.com for more information.

EMBRACING UNCERTAINTY AND ANXIETY

Robert H. Rosen

Whether your leadership position is new for you or not, you face unprecedented change and uncertainty these days. Constant change is the new norm—its pace excruciatingly hard on businesses. You may be struggling to keep up with changing global markets, economic uncertainties, disruptive technologies, or demanding customers. You may be contending with mergers, acquisitions, growth, or downsizing. The uncertainty created by so much change makes your job challenging at best.

Complexity and change also offer you unprecedented opportunities. They enable you to grow as an individual and in business. But it's not easy. Constant change places you in a continual state of transformation and is unsettling, unnerving, and intimidating. It creates anxiety, making you feel vulnerable, uneasy, and helpless. Living with change creates gap after gap after gap between your current reality and your desired future.

Let's face it: Leadership used to be about creating certainty. Now it is about leading through uncertainty. Anxiety has become a constant companion. How you use it makes all the difference. If you let it overwhelm you, it will turn to panic. If you deny or run from it, you will become complacent. But if you use anxiety in a positive way, you will turn it into a powerful force in your life—your hidden driver of business success.

Success today requires understanding and accepting three basic realities:

- It's time to embrace change, uncertainty, and anxiety as facts of life.

- You can use healthy anxiety as a positive force for growth.

- Maintaining just enough anxiety is the key to living and leading in today's complex world.

I base these statements on my 30-year career as a psychologist, entrepreneur, and CEO adviser, and from interviewing and working with 250 top business leaders at a variety of top firms, including GlaxoSmithKline, Johnson & Johnson, Northrop Grumman, Intel, PricewaterhouseCoopers, Boeing, and ING.

What is just enough anxiety? It is the exact amount of anxiety that you need to respond to danger, tackle a tough problem, or take a leap of faith. It is the right amount for *you,* given the person you are and what motivates you. Healthy anxiety is the right level of arousal that, combined with the right attitude, enables you to optimize your performance. It makes you *want* to do better, to stretch beyond your current reality into your desired future.

Reprinted from Leader to Leader Number 50, Fall 2008

With just enough anxiety, you can embrace uncertainty and turn burning platforms into opportunities: you can mobilize people and optimize performance. You can drive meaningful change throughout your organization. But how do you create just enough anxiety within yourself and in others?

Lead with an Open Mind and an Open Heart

Leading change requires an open mind. Without that, you remain a slave to the past, easily hijacked by your fear of anxiety—or by anxiety itself—which limits your ability to navigate through uncertainty. You stand still. In this era of constant and continual change, that's not acceptable.

An open mind allows you to see where you're going and understand the terrain and roadblocks along the way. It enables you to understand yourself and others extremely well. With an open mind you can face challenges with insight and courage. You can embrace growth and change with excitement, inspiration, and resilience.

Three capabilities—self-awareness, lifelong learning, and nonattachment—comprise an open mind. *Self-awareness* forms the foundation for living in uncertainty, enabling you to play to your strengths and compensate for your weaknesses in the midst of change, to read and manage your emotions. *Lifelong learning* feeds the mind and the soul, helping you solve problems and handle adversity, enabling you to grow, to let go of fears and outmoded behaviors. *Nonattachment* involves letting go of your notions about who you are

Complexity and change offer you unprecedented opportunities.

Without an open heart, you remain a slave to the past.

and how things are, freeing you to move beyond negative habits and limiting behavior patterns.

An open heart provides energy needed to move through the gap—from where you are to where you want to be. A leader with an open heart employs three characteristics: emotional honesty, empathy and compassion, and emotional resilience. *Emotional honesty* provides people with an atmosphere in which they can express their feelings, freely and flexibly. It opens the path to progress for both leaders and their teams, serving to turn the energy of emotions into productive energy. *Empathy and compassion* are the emotions that allow people not only to understand other people's feelings but also to identify with, and honor, those feelings. Empathic, compassionate leaders provide an environment that maximizes others' sense of well-being while acknowledging and working to minimize others' pain and fear. *Emotional resilience* is the ability to navigate and recover from the inevitable emotional ups and downs of life. As in the lyrics of an old popular song, it is what enables you "to pick yourself up, dust yourself off, and start all over again."

Rand Construction founder and CEO Linda Rabbit is a role model for open mind and open heart leadership. Heading one of the top women-owned construction companies in the country, Rabbit is deeply self-aware and aware of others, seeing things for what they are, while envisioning what they can be.

"I'm willing to live with a lot of uncertainty in the quest for being better tomorrow than I was yesterday," Rabbit says. Yet, aware that her level of comfort with change can create anxiety for others, she constantly monitors the anxiety in her organization. "If I see certain behaviors happening around here, I can pretty much predict what's going on and what I need to fix." She helps people manage their anxiety by listening to them, openly acknowledging their accomplishments, and being honest about her own frailties. "If I set the bar really high, and I look and act like I'm perfect, it doesn't do anyone any good. I have to be human. So I tell stories about ways that I've failed. When you have high expectations, you're not going to always achieve them. Sometimes you're going to fall on your face."

Master Three Key Leadership Paradoxes

Leaders who live with just enough anxiety are masters at living in three paradoxes: realistic optimism, constructive impatience, and confident humility. Their ability to balance these seemingly opposing qualities enables them to create just enough anxiety within themselves and their organizations. A paradox exists when two opposing but complementary ideas contain equal power or truth. Both sides of a paradox are real although contradictory to each other—like positive and negative, or dark and light. Sometimes one dominates, sometimes the other.

Realistic optimism involves telling the truth about the present while dreaming the future. Being realistic is all about seeking and speaking the truth—starting with being honest about who you are: your strengths and shortcomings, hopes and fears, triumphs and failures. It involves knowing how people see you, and how you affect them. Being optimistic is all about dreaming the

future—believing that tomorrow will be better than today. Realistic optimists ask for feedback and are not afraid of what they will hear. They listen deeply to what people say, while observing their behavior, picking up on their feelings, and assessing their intentions. People know they can count on realistic optimists to tell it like it is and to follow through on their commitments.

This ability to balance optimism and realism is at the heart of Gary Hirschberg's success. The Stonyfield Farms founder and CEO turned $500 and seven Jersey cows into a $250 million organic yogurt business. "Don't let folks tell you it can't be done. There's always a way if you believe in it enough," he says.

A passionate dreamer, Hirschberg also understands that the day-to-day realities of business have to be faced head-on. And he knows that reality can be harsh. Quoting Lily Tomlin, he quips, "'Reality is the leading cause of stress for those who are in touch with it.' There's nothing easy about business, and I struggle every single day. One principle that works for me is to be brutally honest about what's going on—what we do well and what we don't do well, and where our work is still unfinished."

Constructive impatience involves engaging people and making it psychologically safe for them to take risks, while challenging them to higher and higher levels of performance, stretching beyond what seems possible. Leading with constructive impatience is a lot like pulling a rubber band. If you pull too hard, you break people's spirits. If you don't pull hard enough, you fail to maximize their potential. But if you find the right tension, amazing things happen. You engage people's hearts and minds and create just enough anxiety to stretch them to their limits—and beyond.

Cadbury Schweppes CEO Todd Stitzer knows that his ability to stretch people beyond their limits in a constructive way is the key to achieving his goal. When I spoke to Stitzer in London, he told me this story: "When I became CEO, I challenged people to make the company and themselves the very best they could be. Cadbury Schweppes competes with giants—like Nestlé, with nearly $69 billion in sales, and Coke with $24 billion. Being among the best, feeling that you've

> *"Reality is the leading cause of stress for those who are in touch with it."*

danced with elephants and avoided being stomped on, appeals to a lot of people. So I set a goal to be a top-quartile performer in our industry."

Stitzer continually resets the rules of the game. Shortly after he became CEO in 2003, Cadbury Schweppes made its largest acquisition, Adams. Stitzer created just enough anxiety in his team to decrease the time frame for a new Adams product, first moving the bar from the original 24 to 36 months to 9 to 18 months, then to 6 to 14 months. He says, "And they did. We out-innovated Wrigley in 2004, less than two years after the acquisition."

What enables Stitzer to succeed is his ability to live with and create discomfort and excitement inside himself and for the people around him. It's about using constructive impatience to increase buy-in and commitment.

Confident humility involves learning to lead with power and generosity—at the same time. Confidence is an attitude in which you believe in yourself and your ability to master your environment. And it is also about believing in the people around you. It's being sure that your organization can meet challenges head-on, solve problems, and win in the marketplace. Humility enables you to admit that you don't know everything and don't need to know it all. That acknowledgment of your imperfection allows you to build mutually rewarding relationships that champion the strengths and skills in other people that complement your own talents.

At Travelocity, CEO Michelle Peluso consciously blends confidence and humility. Since taking the top spot, she has transformed a company known for cheap airline tickets into one respected for its high-value travel solutions. She says, "If you think you are infallible, you're not learning enough. Still, admitting you're wrong isn't easy. Every time I go through it, it's still painful. But, as a leader, it is sometimes important to acknowledge it publicly." She recalls the time when two technology teams had different outcomes. One missed its milestone, the other team delivered. Upon investigation, Peluso learned that the "delivery team" had taken the easy way to complete its assignment, while the other team had held to a higher quality standard. What did she do? She says, "Basically, I had rewarded the team that

When you are wrong, it is important to acknowledge it publicly.

took no risk. And that's obviously not what I should be doing. When I found out, I was very public about it. 'I blew it,' I said. 'I should have looked deeper.'" Peluso is confidently comfortable with herself, her strengths and vulnerabilities—and humbly, sometimes painfully truthfully, uses and rewards the strengths of others. She understands the power of confident humility.

Getting It Wrong, Getting It Right

Former Qwest CEO Joe Nacchio created *too much anxiety* and nearly upended the company with his cowboy mentality and combative leadership style. Nacchio seemed like the perfect leader for Qwest at the beginning of the telecom revolution—his tough-guy style served the small company well as it went up against the big-timers. But when the industry playing field leveled somewhat, Nacchio didn't modify his style or abandon his obsession with winning, He was very clearly "all about the bottom line." "The most important thing we do is meet our numbers," he said in an employee meeting. "It's more important than any individual product, individual philosophy, or individual cultural change we're making. We stop everything else when we don't make the numbers." To please him, his employees inflated revenue. Eventually, Qwest was charged with fraudulently reporting $3 billion in revenue: Nacchio landed in prison.

While at Vivendi, CEO Jean Pierre Messier created *too little anxiety* with his unfounded belief that everything would work out okay no matter what he did. Early on, he catapulted Vivendi from deep losses to astounding growth. He went on a buying binge to diversify the

You will have discovered the hidden driver to business success.

company, but he underestimated the magnitude of risk and overestimated his ability to navigate through a complex marketplace. He believed so much in himself and his ability to work things out favorably that he created too little anxiety in himself and the company. When he resigned, Messier's company was only ten days away from bankruptcy, having reported the largest one-year loss in French corporate history.

Without just enough anxiety, you will not be able to navigate the gaps between your current status and your desired outcome successfully.

But if you succeed in leading with an open mind and an open heart, if you master the three key paradoxes of realistic optimism, constructive impatience, and confident humility, you will turn anxiety into productive energy. You will mobilize people and optimize performance. You will build a winning, flexible, adaptive organization. You will be a leader who uses just enough anxiety as a positive and powerful force in your life and in your organization. You will have discovered the hidden driver to business success.

Robert H. Rosen is a psychologist, popular keynote speaker, and the CEO of Healthy Companies International, an executive consulting and education firm. In his 30-year career, he has interviewed and worked with more than 250 top business leaders at leading companies throughout the world. Rosen is the author of "Just Enough Anxiety: The Hidden Driver of Business Success." His prior books include "Global Literacies: Lessons on Business Leadership and National Cultures," "Leading People: Transforming Business from the Inside Out," and "The Healthy Company: Eight Strategies to Develop People, Productivity, and Profits." For more information visit www.justenoughanxiety.com or www .healthycompanies.com.

THE ART OF ASKING FOR HELP

by Nora Klaver

Walter was at a loss. This was the third time in the last two years he had been taken to task for micromanaging his team. Each time he had tried to do things differently—without success. Making it worse, Walter had just learned that he wasn't going to be promoted to senior vice president. Walter wanted help, but he wouldn't admit that he couldn't solve this problem on his own.

As an executive coach to Fortune 500 companies, I have seen Walter's scenario happen frequently—and I'm not talking about the micromanaging. Instead, what intrigues me is how frequently executives and staff wait too long to ask for the help they need. They delay their requests for help until it is too late.

When reality finally hits, it hits hard.

In 2007, I conducted a survey of executives and senior managers in the Chicago area—the results were sobering. Within this group of leaders, 44 percent admitted they would either *never* ask for help at work, or only do so as an absolute last resort. Moreover, 70 percent said they'd *wanted to ask for help in the previous week, but didn't.* Clearly, Walter isn't alone.

Consider the publishing manager who pushed herself to drive (with manual transmission no less) alone from Los Angeles to San Francisco with her right leg in a cast, the new technology VP who was less experienced than the team she was assigned to lead, or the advertising president trying to acclimate to a new company culture. Each has a legitimate need that could have been resolved had they only asked for help.

Failure to ask for help has very real costs, as documented in the sidebar, "The Cost of Not Asking for Help." In Walter's case, his refusal to ask for help was costing him and his company—big. His direct reports were demoralized and underutilized. Staff complaints about Walter's approach to management consumed valuable time. Walter spent his time on the wrong things. Sadly, Walter's time and effort in "fixing" the problem also seemed wasted. Walter had to swallow his pride so his career and the company's investment could be salvaged.

The last thing many of us want to do is to make a request for help. Rather than risk exposing ourselves, we work doubly hard to hide the gaps—our needs. Some deny that they have needs at all. Most of us even go so far as to refuse assistance when it is offered us. "Nah, that's okay, I got it covered," is a refrain I often hear—even when it is obvious that "it" has not been covered at all. In the meantime, we try to "work smarter" or perhaps longer. Finally, when nothing changes, we hit that wall of desperation. We find

Reprinted from Leader to Leader Number 49, Summer 2008

ourselves ready to do what we had long avoided—ask for help.

Why Don't We Ask?

Why do we avoid asking for what we need? Why do we wait so long? Cultural reasons are at play, of course. Americans value independence and the very idea of being reliant on another is often untenable. Self-sufficiency is the order of the day and the century. It's more than a desire to fit into society. These external cultural pressures just reinforce what is going on inside our own heads: fear.

Ultimately, fear is what stops us from asking for what we need. Three key fears in particular shut our mouths and stop us from forming the request. The *fear of separation* comes to mind first. We may refer to it as the fear of rejection, but it is more than that. Some of us don't ask for help because we don't believe we can bear that feeling of rejection. Separation from others is what we really dread. (Remember that banishment was historically considered a fate worse than or on par with death.) It is emotionally painful to be singled out or separated from our work communities, families, or

"Nah, that's okay, I got it covered!" But do you?

friends. In a fear-riddled mind, rejection of a request equates to rejection of the entire self. In despair or panic-mode, we have a hard time telling the difference.

Walter was only partly worried about rejection or separation. This had been his third trip to the woodshed with his boss. He was sure she would reject his request for more help. She'd spent too much time on him already—or at least that's what his fear was telling him. Poor Walter also feared a different kind of separation, that of being fired over his behavior problem. Forcibly losing a job is the ultimate kind of separation at work.

Fear of surrender and loss of control is the second worry that stops us from asking for what we need. Loss of control was Walter's greatest concern. Walter wanted

THE COST OF NOT ASKING FOR HELP

There is a very real cost when leaders don't ask for help when they should, and instead forge ahead on their own. In addition to a personal toll that these men and women pay in lost hours and overwork, a price is also paid by the organization. Here is a short list of possible repercussions.

Increased costs. Not asking means a team of others may have to be pulled at the last moment to assist and meet a critical deadline. This is usually a costly fix for a problem that might have been resolved relatively easily earlier.

Decreased team efficiency. Not asking means employees waste time on tasks that might have been resolved more quickly with the aid of another.

Reduced overall productivity. Not asking means team member skills, talents, and capabilities are not used to the fullest.

Limited development of others. Not asking means we don't give others an opportunity to grow, learn, and shine.

Limited team bonding. Not asking creates weak ties between team members. Helping one another strengthens a team.

Unrealistic expectations. Not asking sets unrealistic expectations for our colleagues to do the same.

Elimination of authenticity in the workplace. Not asking is like keeping a secret—one that impacts everyone else. Keeping it real at work means admitting to and accepting each other's, and our own, needs.

to control not only the work product but the work process as well. He did what he could to avoid surrendering to the skills, talents, and capabilities of his peers and direct reports. He knew that if he asked his team to help, he might have to relinquish control, something he'd rarely done before. This is a common concern. Twenty-six percent of those queried indicated that, when requesting help, they feared losing control over the situation.

Surrender also might mean having to fork over a known or unknown price for any help rendered. Many dread being indebted to another or having to reciprocate in the future. Being beholden, even for a favor, means a loss of control. For example, Jin, a senior business analyst, prided herself on always being there for others. She told me she never asked for help. "I don't want to feel like I owe someone something, like someone has something on me."

Finally, the *fear of shame* is the most widely reported reason for not asking for that helping hand. My survey indicated that over 55 percent of the respondents were most concerned about looking weak, needy, stupid, or incompetent when asking for help. When we ask for help, we inadvertently reveal something unflattering about ourselves. We work hard to keep those shadow behaviors (as defined by Carl Jung) in the dark. Exposure might leave us ashamed. This fear of shame was at the root of Walter's micromanagement. He was certain others would perceive him as a weak leader if he wasn't on top of every detail. When it came to asking for help, he believed it would clearly demonstrate that he was too incompetent to lead a team.

Unfortunately, when we delay asking for help, there is a greater chance that the very consequences we fear most—rejection, loss of control, shame—will all come true. The longer we prolong problems, the worse they

Self-sufficiency is the order of the day and the century.

The longer we prolong problems, the worse they get.

get. When Walter delayed getting help because he didn't want to be rejected, lose control, or look incompetent, that's exactly what happened to him.

Creating Supportive Work Environments

So what's a leader to do? How do we help those who are too terrified to admit they need help? We need to take our teams a step further and create a truly supportive work environment. Employees need to believe that not only is it expected to give help to one another, it is permissible to ask for it when needed. Here are a few suggestions to foster requests for help in your company:

Use the language of help. In researching this area of leaders who don't ask for help, I found that there are few synonyms for the word *help*. Perhaps it is because help is such an uncomfortable topic that we never bothered creating new words or phrases to describe it. Nevertheless, the word *help* is incredibly powerful. It immediately elicits emotions of compassion, kindness, consideration, and sympathy. It conveys that you are open to the assistance of others. Those who ask for help recognize their own capabilities and truly value the contributions of others.

The more comfortable we are with the words "I need your help," the more comfortable others will be. Use the words, even while delegating. Tell your direct reports, "I need your help on this." The message is subtle, but it still conveys your need and their part in satisfying it.

Walter used the word *help* to resolve his dilemma and to prove to himself that it was okay to ask for it.

Though he had characteristically overprepared for his team meetings in Europe, I encouraged him to discard any work he had already completed. Giggling with nervousness as he ripped up documents, Walter agreed. I challenged him to ask his new teams for help with agenda setting, planning, and identifying key deliverables. Walter doubted the effectiveness of this approach, but he went along with the script.

After the meeting, Walter called me from the Berlin airport. He was ecstatic. "This was great! I was incredibly nervous and my hands were shaking, but I asked for their help. They all stepped up and pitched in. Not only that, they were involved and excited about what we were doing together. So am I!"

Reward requests for help. Companies like GE and 3M celebrate failures as well as successes. The same principle can be applied here. Reward not only those who give assistance, but those who ask for it as well. At status meetings, point out how one team asked another for staffing help. Spotlight someone who asked for your help—giving you a chance to remember that a need vocalized by one person may really reflect the unspoken needs of the group. Celebrate the courage of the request.

Encourage awareness. Train your people to pay attention to each other. Look for distress signals or signs of being overwhelmed. Notice when someone is looking disheveled or simply exhausted. Track the number of sick days or requests for time off. Ask questions of your staff and really listen to the responses. Do emotions match words? Are they saying they are excited about the next project, but their voices sound flat and tired? These distress signals may indicate an unspoken need that could be easily resolved with a little help.

Calculate the costs of not asking. The next time you find out that someone didn't ask for help until it was too late, calculate the cost to the organization for their delayed request. Without embarrassing the culprit, share the data with your teams. Explain the bottom-line result of not asking for the help they need.

Reflect on your own behavior. Ask yourself what it is you may be doing to perpetuate these key fears in your work environment. Were you welcoming the last time someone asked you for help? Did you exact a price that might have been too rigorous? Have you ever ridiculed someone for asking for help? Be honest with yourself. Determine how your leadership sets the tone.

Were you welcoming the last time someone asked you for help?

Bring help into status meetings. Add an item to meeting agendas: Requests for Help. Brainstorm how each team member might need assistance that week. Talk about it openly and then brainstorm possible solutions. As a group, discover how easy asking for help can be.

Plan for help. Show your people how to plan the request. Determine, as best you can, the need to be met. Identify the usual suspects and then expand the list to include other people who might be willing and able to contribute. Get clear on your request before you make it. Nothing is worse than asking someone for help and realizing later that they didn't understand what you meant at all. With your helper, determine when the help is to be rendered, how it should be completed, and who else might be involved. Agree on how you will work with each other to complete the task. Treat your request as a conversation, not just a plea for help.

Use humor. My clients tend to exaggerate problems, making them more significant than they actually are. This "significance" actually works to worsen the situation, making it more difficult to address. The problem, which may have been quite small, will have grown quite large, at least in their eyes. One way to knock it back down to size is to use humor. Laughing at your dilemma makes it easier to request help. Even Walter's giggling put his own requests into perspective.

Be cooperative, not competitive. Karlin Sloan and Co., a consulting firm dedicated to developing sustainable leadership, has created unusual business relationships where requests for help are regularly traded back and forth. The interesting thing is that these relationships are with KS&C competitors. Their agreement is to work with each other to find opportunities to sell and deliver services. The understanding is that if a group of coaches needs help with a client, they can call on KS&C, and vice versa. Their open requests for help keep both companies strong and thriving.

A Time to Jump

Will you create a monster by encouraging others to ask for help—someone who uses others indiscriminately to get their own work done? Highly unlikely. Others will catch on quickly. Ultimately, though, few people become expert at admitting their needs and requesting help. Thousands of years of evolution and subtle fears stop us from reaching out for that helping hand.

But if we can simply ask for help 10 or 20 percent more often than we do now, the costs to our companies and ourselves will diminish equally. We might even discover surprising benefits such as tighter teams, clearer communication, more efficient work processes, and better work product. As Carl Jung once said, "If there is a fear of falling, the only safety consists in deliberately jumping."

So my suggestion to you is to jump.

M. Nora Klaver is a Chicago-based work-life expert and author of "Mayday! Asking for Help in Times of Need" (Berrett-Koehler, 2007). An executive coach with twenty years of experience, she advises both individuals and corporate leaders at organizations from Allstate Financial to American Movie Classics. Contact her on the Web at maydaythebook.com.

THE POWER

OF

ACCOUNTABILITY

Linda Galindo

A team of employees is preparing to make an important presentation to a new customer—one that your company is banking on for its future growth. If the presentation goes well and the customer agrees to a contract for the work, your business will just barely show a profit this year—not bad in this down economy. If the presentation does not go well, however, and this prospective customer doesn't sign a new contract, then your company will be on track for a major loss for the year. Severe cost cuts—including layoffs—will be necessary to minimize the financial damage.

As the team is preparing to leave their hotel and catch a cab to the client's main offices, a call comes in from the marketing assistant back at the home office three time zones away. The marketing assistant has just discovered that the team has the wrong PowerPoint presentation.

The sales representative takes the call and a heated discussion ensues. "What do you mean it's the wrong presentation?" objects the sales rep, "I put it together myself! Are you telling me I don't know what I'm doing?"

The marketing assistant then calls the office of the vice president of marketing, hoping that she will do something to intercede. The vice president's assistant takes the call. "Sorry, but she can't be bothered right now. She's in a very important meeting." As the team jumps in their cab, the marketing assistant gives up and decides to go to lunch.

Which one of these people is responsible for the PowerPoint presentation? Is it the sales representative whose job it is to load it into the computer? Is it the marketing assistant, who gave the PowerPoint file to the sales representative before the team flew out to the prospective customer's location? Is it the vice president's assistant, who could have put the marketing assistant's call through to her boss? Or is it the vice president of marketing, who promised the prospective customer that his team would dazzle them but didn't know that there was a problem?

You get a call from the customer, who is not happy with the way the presentation went. There will be no contract. Who will you hold accountable? The sales representative? He thought he had the right PowerPoint presentation. The marketing assistant? He tried to get the right presentation to the team. The vice president's assistant? The presentation wasn't her job. The vice president of marketing? She had no idea there was a problem.

Again, if just one of these people is responsible, does that mean that none of the others are accountable?

Should the others also be held accountable to some degree for this failure?

If your company wants to stay in business—yes.

The Accountability Gap

There is a major problem in business today—a serious lack of accountability and personal responsibility. You can observe it for yourself any time an employee blames someone else, or some other organization—or simply "the system"—after failing to achieve a goal or complete an assignment. To get a better sense of the problem, ask yourself and your people the following question:

How much of your success is up to you, and how much of it is determined by outside conditions, like the environment, other people, or just plain bad luck?

Your answer—and the answers you get from your people—speak volumes. If you said fifty-fifty, or anything less than 85 percent, you almost certainly blame your problems and failures—big or small, personal or professional—on other people, "circumstances beyond my control," or just plain bad luck. And why not? All of us face countless obstacles each and every day, and these obstacles conspire against achieving the goals we set for ourselves and for others.

But what if I told you that in my work with hundreds of executives that the most successful men and women—in business and in life in general—aren't satisfied with this answer? The data they provide on our validated Accountability Assessment shows it over and over again; they are convinced that at minimum, 85 percent or more of their success is up to the actions they themselves take, and that only 15 percent or less is due to outside conditions or other people. They know that when outside obstacles get in their way, they are ultimately responsible for deciding how to deal with these obstacles to find a path around them.

Whatever you may think of Jack Welch's management legacy at General Electric, there can be no doubt that his steadfast focus on providing shareholder value made the company one of the most successful in the world during his tenure at the top. Welch achieved

Choose accountability and own your personal success and happiness.

this by creating a culture where risk was rewarded and accountability and measurable goals were most important. As Jack Welch once said, "Face reality as it is, not as it was or as you wish it to be."

The 85 Percent Solution—Three Steps to Owning Your Success

So what if the answer to the question in the preceding section is something less than 85 percent? Should you and your people accept this outcome and stick with business as usual? In today's economy, actually, in *any* economy, the answer is clearly and unequivocally NO. Instead, I challenge you to choose accountability and own your personal success and happiness. It's not as easy as one-two-three, but it is a three-part process.

Responsibility

Responsibility is not something you do—it's a way of thinking and being. When you're truly responsible, you believe that success or failure is up to you, even if you work within a team or are blindsided by unforeseen circumstances. You own your commitment to a result before the fact—before you even take action. Getting started:

Be responsible either way. It's easy to claim responsibility when things go well, but it's hard when they don't. A truly responsible person or team, however, is responsible either way. So next time you take on a project, be 100 percent responsible for the outcome. Not a little. Not somewhat. Not pretty much. Not "I guess so" or "as long as." Own it 100 percent—good or bad—with no wiggle room.

Recognize your power. You already have the ability to be 100 percent responsible—everybody does. Yet most of us don't realize—or at least don't admit—that we alone have the power to manage our lives and careers. Sure, you can give that power away, but that is a conscious choice—it doesn't happen without your permission.

Deal with what *is*. When was the last time you were able to change the past? Truth is, it doesn't matter what *should* have happened—it matters what *is*. That saves you the trouble of figuring out who's to blame or worrying about how things "coulda woulda shoulda" been if only something had gone differently. It didn't—and that makes your choice a cinch: "How do I want to react to the situation that is?"

Self-Empowerment

There is only one kind of empowerment, and that is *self*-empowerment. Unlike authority, empowerment comes from within. By empowering yourself, you take the actions—and the risks—to achieve a result and get what you want. Rather than waiting for someone to declare you empowered or give you that one lucky break, you step outside your comfort zone, make things happen, and answer for the outcomes. Getting started:

Manage expectations. The most direct route to self-empowerment is to be clear about expectations—not only what you expect, but also what's expected of you. To do that, you need to ask questions, make agreements, and clarify everything in writing. Otherwise, you risk suffering the source of all upset: missed expectations.

Take back your time. "No" is an empowering word. So every time you find yourself thinking, "I can't say

When was the last time you were able to change the past?

"No" is an empowering word.

no," ask yourself if you can't—or if you're unwilling to. Take back your time in other ways, too: get rid of your to-do list (track projects and deadlines on a calendar instead); resist overscheduling (you can't cram 12 hours of work into 8 hours, so stop trying); and estimate realistically (let's face it, most everything takes longer than we think).

Sing your own praises. It's an all-too-common workplace mantra: "One day they'll notice how much I do around here and give me the recognition I deserve." NOT! Take stock of your personal talents and triumphs and let the higher-ups know who you are and what you contribute.

Personal Accountability

Unlike responsibility (the *before*) and self-empowerment (the *during*), personal accountability is the *after*. It's a willingness—after all is said and done—to answer for the outcomes of your choices, actions, and behaviors. When you're personally accountable, you stop assigning blame, "should-ing" on people, and making excuses. Instead, you take the fall when your choices cause problems. Getting started:

Tell the truth. Everybody messes up sometimes. Lying about it or trying to cover it up always makes it worse—no exceptions. Save yourself some time: Don't tell untruths. Nobody believes them anyway—not even you.

Police yourself. Are you accountable for your actions even if nobody holds you accountable—or nobody catches you? You bet you are. So be your own "Accountability Cop" and police yourself. On the long and winding road of life, choose accountability at every turn.

Choose accountability at every turn.

Look to yourself—first. When trouble arises, look first to yourself. Ask four specific questions: "What is the problem?" "What am I doing—or not doing—to contribute to the problem?" "What will I do differently to help solve the problem?" and "How will I be accountable for the result?"

Are You an Accountable Leader?

We all know intuitively that the problem of low personal accountability starts individually, but for leaders, consider that leadership is a bankrupt concept without personal accountability; we are fooling ourselves not to see it. Instead of saying "the company lost money this quarter" the leader would say "I posted a loss this quarter and here is how I am accountable for it." No accountability, no trust. No trust, no confidence. And no confidence results in people keeping their money or hoping things will change.

It is only true leadership if you are accountable—you answer for your results good or bad without fault, blame, or guilt. If you are a leader, is it position power or leadership by accountability? You can only demonstrate accountability, not mandate it. The workforce and the public are starved for examples so we can choose to work for and buy from accountable companies.

Are you an accountable leader? If you are, what's your story? And if you are not one, when will you start and what will you do? The most important thing to keep in mind if you want accountability in your world is that it starts at the top—and you are the top.

Linda Galindo is an accountability expert and author of "The 85% Solution: How Personal Accountability Guarantees Success—No Nonsense, No Excuses." Founder and president of Galindo Consulting, Inc., she advises CEOs, leadership teams, and boards of directors in making personal accountability their organizations' central organizing principle. She is a faculty member of the Governance Institute, Medical Leadership Institute, and Institute for Management Studies, and a board member of the Center for the Public Trust of the National Association of State Boards of Accountancy (NASBA). Contact her on the Web at lindagalindo.com.

ABOUT DALE CARNEGIE TRAINING®

Dale Carnegie partners with middle market and large corporations, as well as organizations, to produce measurable business results by improving the performance of employees with emphasis on:

- leadership
- sales
- customer service
- presentations
- team member engagement
- process improvement

Recently identified by *The Wall Street Journal* as one of the top 25 high-performing franchises, Dale Carnegie Training programs are available in more than 25 languages throughout the entire United States and in more than 80 countries.

Dale Carnegie's corporate specialists work with individuals, groups and organizations to design solutions that unleash your employees' potential, enabling your organization to reach the next level of performance. Dale Carnegie Training offers public courses, seminars and workshops, as well as in-house customized training, corporate assessments, online reinforcement and one-on-one coaching.

For more information, please visit www.dalecarnegie.com.

CUSTOMIZED CORPORATE SOLUTIONS:
YOUR PLAN. OUR TOOLS. BUILDING YOUR SUCCESS.

iMAP
THE ROAD THAT GETS YOU WHERE YOU WANT TO GO

intent ← Your organization's strategic vision - the "should be" as opposed to the "as is".

inquire ← A strategic conversation with you to understand where the operation is today, where you want to take it and what needs to change to get there.

involve ← Through assessments, surveys and a unique BID process, determine the alignment around the vision, competency gaps that need to be closed, and attitudes that undermine change.

innovate ← Design interventions that support your strategic intent, provide measurable results, map directly to the competencies needed to power the strategic intent, blend competency development with attitudinal change and align emotional intelligence with corporate initiatives.

impact ← Ingrain long-term behavior change to gain emotional and intellectual engagement with corporate objectives.

In addition to the full programs listed on our website, we also have an ever-increasing library of configurable modules that can be used to align interventions with your business drivers.

Any of the programs on our website or the configurable modules listed he be customized to fit your unique needs using the iMap process.
CALL YOUR LOCAL OFFICE FOR DETAILS.

TEAM MEMBER ENGAGEMENT
- Internal Conflict Resolution
- Conflict – Maintaining Emotional Control
- Conflict Mediation
- Conflict as a Growth Opportunity
- Bringing Conflict into the Open
- Conflict to Collaboration
- Establishing an Effective Team
- Being a Contributing Team Member
- Team Building
- Dealing with Difficult Team Members
- Ending a Successful Team
- External Partnerships
- Communicate with Diplomacy & Tact
- Team Building Basics
- Work with Difficult People
- Emotional Control
- Negotiations: A Human Relations Approach
- Avoid Burnout
- Balance Work and Life
- Interpersonal Competence: Connect with Others
- Interpersonal Competence for Career Growth
- Keep Stress and Worry in Perspective
- Understanding Diversity
- Valuing Diversity
- Communicating Across Generations
- Understanding Generational Diversity
- Stress Reduction through New Work Habits
- Disagree Agreeably
- Foundation for Success

- Interpersonal Competence: Enhance Teamwork
- Interpersonal Competence: Influence Change
- Interpersonal Competence: Best Practices
- Sustaining Measurable Success
- Leveraging Diversity
- Managing Across Generations
- Staying Positive in the Face of Layoffs

LEADERSHIP DEVELOPMENT
- Delegation
- Planning
- Performance Appraisals
- Motivation
- Performance Defined
- Vision, Mission, and Values
- Time Management
- Handling Mistakes
- Conflict Management
- Time Control to Work on Your Business
- Coaching–Supportive and Directive Approaches
- Leading Strong Teams
- Lead Effective Meetings
- New Employee Orientation
- Communicate to Lead
- Business Professionalism 101
- Global Travel and Culture
- Strategic Planning
- Ethical Leadership
- Succession Planning
- Network through Community Service
- Focus and Discipline
- Leadership Communications
- Leadership Styles and Tendencies

- Motivational Leadership
- Share the Glory
- Visionary Leadership
- Mentorship - Launching an Initiative
- Build Trust, Credibility, and Respect
- Multi-Tasking
- Networking to Build Your Personal Brand
- Networking to Promote Your Organization
- Coach for Performance Improvement
- Mentorship: Creating a Partnership
- Network to Build Business Connections

PRESENTATION EFFECTIVENESS
- Planning Presentations
- Vocal Skills and Body Language
- Team Presentations
- Confrontational Questions
- Presenting with Visual Impact
- Present to Persuade
- Present to Gain Input
- Present to Inform
- Facilitate for Group Results

PROCESS IMPROVEMENT
- Innovation
- Team Problem Solving and Decision Making
- Process Improvement
- Adjust to Change
- Analyze Problems and Make Decisions
- Change Engagement

- Manage Change Effectively
- Team Change Engagement
- Lead Change without Authority
- Project Planning

SALES EFFECTIVENESS
- Successful Sales Leadership
- Sales Performance Defined
- Sales Meetings
- Coaching Salespeople
- Recruiting Salespeople
- Rapport
- Interest
- Solution
- Objections
- Motive and Commitment
- Hiring Salespeople
- Master the Selling Process
- Uncover Selling Opportunities
- Foundation for Consultative Selling

CUSTOMER SERVICE
- Attitudes for Service
- Complaint Resolution
- Cross and Up Selling
- Internal Customer Service
- Manage Customer Expectation
- Generate Customer Interest
- Create Loyal Customers
- Effective First Impressions: Fac to Face
- Customer Follow Through
- Customer Value Solutions
- Referrals
- Service to Sales
- Suggestion Selling
- Telephone Skills: Inbound and Outbound